1920, Shots Fired, Officer Down

"Stan Cook is one of those rare individuals who have dedicated his life to serving not only his country but also the citizens of Honolulu. His service in the Navy and combat experience well prepared him for duty as a Honolulu Police Officer as it came apparent on 31 August 1994 when he survived a gun fight with an individual intent on killing a police officer. This is his story of not giving up the fight to live another day. I'm proud to call him my friend. Well-told Stan. Semper Fi."

Larry Groah, SgtMajor USMC (ret) *(http://sgtmajgroah.com)*

"A very interesting and informative read. I learned a lot about the author, my dad, of what he went through before, during and after the shooting. Putting his experience on paper to share with the world benefits us all."

Emi Santaella

"Overall, I like it. It tells an interesting story, it's you and it's fascinating.

Stephen Bloch *(http://stephenbloch.com)*

"It's a solid story. I think you have another book in you."

Gerald Menefee *(http://submarinehistoricnovels.com/)*

1920, Shots Fired, Officer Down. HPD Officer Stan Cook

HONOLULU POLICE OFFICER STAN COOK

1920, Shots Fired, Officer Down

Officer Stan Cook survives 8 hits from a an AK-47.

THE WHOLE STORY

1920, Shots Fired, Officer Down

Printed in the United States of America
ISBN-978-0-9888126-1-1

Learn more information at:
http://www.theshooting.com
1

Contents

Table of Contents

Prologue ii

Chapter 1 Going to Hawaii 1

Chapter 2 Police Academy 3

Chapter 3 Police Rookie..11

Chapter 4 Working Towards Solo Bike 19

Chapter 5 Solo Bike Training 25

Chapter 6 August 31, 1994.....................................32

Chapter 7 The Incident..35
    THE SHOOTING 37

Chapter 8 The Aftermath..48
    Recovery Number Two Begins: 61

Chapter 9 Samoans And Their Culture 67

Chapter 10 Hawaii, you will always have to come home...72

Epilogue - Lessons Learned 74

About the Author...85

1920, Shots Fired, Officer Down. HPD Officer Stan Cook

ACKNOWLEDGMENTS

This book is dedicated to my wife, Fe Cook. She never asked for this, but found a strength she never knew she had. I could not have asked for a better partner in life than Fe. I am a very lucky man in more ways than one.

Thanks to Gerald Menefee, Steve Bloch, Larry Groah and my daughter, Emi Santaella for their time in proofreading this book. It is true that you can never proofread your own writings.

Prologue

I joined the Honolulu Police Department in February 1989. After passing many tests I was admitted to the 103rd Honolulu Police Department Academy class. At that time I was forty-nine years old and a retired military veteran married to Fe Geraldo Cook. Fe and I were married in 1981 while I was working as a radio Deejay at a Honolulu top forty station KIKI[1].

While attending the police academy I had several occasions to see solo bikers ride onto the academy campus. A solo bike [2]is what the Honolulu Police Department calls a police motorcycle. Most other states call them motors but in Hawaii they are called solo bikes[2]

---

[1] KIKI AM83 was a top 40 radio station in those days

1920,Shots Fired, Officer Down. HPD Officer Stan Cook
. That is when I decided I wanted to become a Honolulu Police Department Solo Bike Officer.

On August 31, 1994, while on duty I had occasion to conduct a traffic stop on a vehicle with a fraudulent license plate. The result of that traffic stop was I being hit eight times by the driver of that vehicle who was firing an AK47 semi-automatic rifle that fires a .223 Cal [3]bullet. I subsequently killed the subject when I returned fire with my duty weapon, a Smith and Wesson 5906 9MM pistol.

This then is my story.

---

[2] A solo bike is a police motorcycle that only has one rider. In years past HPD had sidecar motorcycle with two riders.
[3] The AK47, normally shoots a 7.62 MM bullet but some were made to shoot the .223 Cal bullet like the US M-16 or AR-15.

Chapter 1 Going to Hawaii

WHILE **ATTENDING** Beaverton Union High School in Beaverton Oregon from 1954 to 1958 I joined the United States Navy Submarine Reserve during my junior year of 1956. Why, you say? Well, it was what most of my friends were doing. After a visit to reserve submarine USS Pargo (SS-264) at the Swan Island Naval Reserve Training Center in Portland, Oregon, I was hooked. In those days, it was not a matter of IF you would join a military organization; it was a matter of which one. Every male had to sign up for the draft at age 18. The only way to avoid some kind of active military duty was to join a National Guard unit. By joining the US Navy Reserve I obligated myself to two years of active duty. We looked at it as an adventure to come.

1

I graduated from high school in June of 1958. In March of 1959 I reported to the US Naval Submarine School in New London, CT. During the nine months before my departure, I worked for The Boeing Company in Seattle, Washington. I really liked Seattle and found I fit in well there. Working at Boeing was great. Even though they knew about my military obligation I was told that I would have a job waiting for me when I returned.

In March of 1959 my high school friend Barry Gilbert and I left Portland, Oregon bound for New London, Connecticut. I attended the submarine school from March to May 1959. After graduating I received orders to the USS Wahoo (SS565) stationed at Pearl Harbor, Hawaii. Thus started my great adventure as a submarine sailor stationed in Hawaii and a future, of course unknown to me at the time, of living in Hawaii for 43 years.

During my 43 years in Hawaii I completed a military career, owned my own electronics business, worked in radio and TV, worked for the Handi Pantry (part of Foodland Corp) and finally, in 1989, joined the Honolulu Police Department.

Chapter 2 Police Academy

IN MID **1988 I** was working as a manager of a Handi Panty store on Date Street in Honolulu's Moiliili District. As I worked days running the store, many times I would have Honolulu police officers stop in for food and drink while working special duty in the area. The more I talked to these officers the more I felt like it was something that I wanted to do.

For many years I had always envied those that were officers. As far back as 1967 I had a friend named Arte Mccollough. He was a TV repairman and was trying to get into the department. He was too short but had himself stretched until he was tall enough to pass. In 1976 I had another friend that was an officer. His name was Bill Morgan and he would tell me a lot about what the job was really like. The only problem was that during these times there was a height requirement. You had to be a certain height minimum and maximum. I, being six foot

3

1920,Shots Fired, Officer Down. HPD Officer Stan Cook four, was too tall. There was also a feeling in those days that if you were not a local you had little chance of getting the job.

Somewhere along the line the Honolulu Police Department adopted the federal non-discrimination laws. They also figured out that hiring ex-military was a good thing. After all, a police department function is based on a military mode. Why not hire those that already have the training. In fact, Honolulu even decided to give extra points to those that had a military background. As far as the physical part was concerned, they decided that age would not be a major factor. What was important was whether you could pass the physical test.

Back then the physical portion of the test was set up in a park near the airport, on a course also used by the Honolulu Fire Department. As I remember it, all the apparatus were painted yellow. Each candidate was required to pull heavy hoses that were supposed to represent a person's body, scale a fence, balance and many more. I took the test and felt good about it. It was really tough but I didn't seem to have that much of a problem with it. I do remember seeing many that were much young than I that could not even finish the course. Needless to say that really helped my confidence. Today that course is long gone. I do know that the park there has been returned to the public.

The first test that we had to take was a written, general knowledge test that was conducted at a grade school cafeteria in Kalihi. It took a couple of hours for that exam. We also had to take a 500 question sociological test, which was conducted in a meeting room in

1920,Shots Fired, Officer Down. HPD Officer Stan Cook
Kapiolani Park. I remember one of the questions was: "When I am standing on top of a high building I feel like I want to jump off." The three possible answers were: Somewhat like me, a lot like me, or not at all like me. Most of the 500 questions in this test had the same three possible answers. The problem is that you have a conflict within your mind as to what you really feel and what you think the answer is that they are looking for. Much later I found out that only a small portion of the questions even counted.

During all this time we also had to submit to a physical examination. It consisted of all the standard things including vision and hearing. Though I wore glasses I was within standards, however, when it came to hearing I had a problem. I flunked the 3,000-Hertz frequencies in my left ear. That is disqualifying. What do I do now? Have I come all this way to be disqualified because I am missing a high frequency in my left ear? Yes, seems that way. But wait; there was one way out. Since the hearing test was done with a city medical examiner I was allowed to seek out a private hearing doctor and let him check my ears. I found one and paid to have the exam done. DAMN! I had the same results there too. Now what? Well, I had insurance with Kaiser so I made an appointment at the Moanalua facility for a hearing test.   One afternoon, I arrived at Kaiser Moanalua and proceeded to the hearing test area. A very nice female doctor met me and I told her my situation. We began the test. I was really trying hard to hear the sound and even anticipate the required response. After it was over she told me that I was close but still below the line for 3,000 Hz. I told her that this was my last chance.

1920,Shots Fired, Officer Down. HPD Officer Stan Cook
I really wanted and needed this job.

"And you will never give me a ticket?" she said.
"Never" I said, with a smile.

She slowly turned to her desk and signed me off.

"I know from your past military training that you will make a good officer," she said as she handed me the paperwork showing that I had passed the hearing test.

"And remember, no tickets," she said.

"Thank you so much Doctor. I won't forget this." I told her as I turned to leave. I have never forgotten what she did and the chance she took. I don't even remember her name but I have always been kind to medical people.

So, there we are, all done with the hard stuff. Well, almost done. The last part of this process is to be interviewed by a "board" consisting of three Honolulu police officers. As I remember it the board was made up of a ranking officer, a sergeant and one other in civilian clothing. I don't remember the questions that were asked but I do remember that it seemed to me that each question was almost a no-win situation. For example, "You are investigating a burglary in a jewelry store. You see one of your fellow officers slip a ring into his pocket. What do you do?" You can see the conflict here. What would I really do and what kind of an answer are they looking for? I have not been trained yet so how am I to know what you should do? Well, I guess they were really just trying to find out what kind of character you have.

6

One of the questions that is always asked of people wanting to become police officers, or even after you enter the academy is: "Why do you want to be a police officer?" Most of the answers are stock like, "I want to serve the public" or "I want to help people" or "I have always wanted to enforce the law." All are good answers and I guess deep down we all feel that way, but I had a different take on it. Though I never told anybody until now, I always had a feeling that essentially you are either a crook and in that "gang" or a cop and in that "gang." I always had a fear of going to jail or prison. I never really broke the law to deserve it and I think most people kind of feel the same. I just wanted to join that gang and be on that side of the fence. In HPD many times we talked about the gangs on the island and always told each other that we ARE the biggest "gang" on the island. We always looked out for each other.

Finally, all was done and now nothing to do but wait. Several weeks later I was contacted by letter that I was accepted and would begin my training with the 103rd Honolulu Police Academy class beginning in February of 1989. It turns out that HPD had selected three classes from all those that took the tests the same time as I did. Also, those with prior military training received extra points. I suppose that might have helped me to be assigned to the first of those three classes.

In February of 1989 I started my adventure as the oldest member of the Honolulu Police Department 103rd recruitclass at Ke Kula Maka'i [4]in Waipahu, Hawaii. Our

---

[4] Ke Kula Maka'i is the name of the Honolulu Police Department training

1920,Shots Fired, Officer Down. HPD Officer Stan Cook class supervisors were Sergeant Robert Imoto and Officer Wayne Kama. I don't remember the number of recruits in our class but on the first morning one of the females was called out of the classroom. Seems as though she had lied about prior traffic tickets or something like that...we never saw her again. I would guess our beginning class size was around 60 or so. We eventually graduated 38.

During our time at Kekula Maka'i we learned HPD rules, Hawaii State law, driving, shooting and first aid including CPR, report writing and much more. Physical fitness was, of course, stressed. At 49 years old I really had to prove myself. I spent a lot of the time before being accepted into HPD working on running and lifting weights. That paid off for the most part. I ended up being in the top one-third of our class for running speed. When it came to lifting weights, however, that was a bit more of a challenge. During our time there we had to reach various levels of fitness. There were three tests we would have to pass. Each test was a bit harder than the last. Lift a little more and run a little faster. The only place I saw I would have a problem was with bench pressing. Each physical level was determined by age, gender and weight. After our second test, which I passed, I began to see that I might have trouble lifting my final weight. I also saw that by losing about 12 pounds I could move myself into a lower level where I knew I could lift the required weight. So, that is what I set out to do by limiting my daily food intake. It worked and I passed my final physical test.

Toward the end of our training we had to pass what they called "Mock Crime Scenes." These were situations

---

academy in Waipahu. Ke Kula meaning school. Maka'i meaning Police.

1920,Shots Fired, Officer Down. HPD Officer Stan Cook played by volunteers, where we were called to the scene and had to perform as if it were the real thing. It could be a robbery, burglary, domestic problem or just a disturbance call. All the scenes were done at the Academy and usually at night. I remember one night I was called to a disturbance of several adults drinking in the park and making noise. I was told that no back up was available. When I got to the area where the adults were I found about 8 of them sitting at a picnic type table. They were making noise but I could not see anyone drinking.

How am I going to handle this, I thought. I am outnumbered and I am not going to get any help in the way of back up.

When I arrived at the table I asked them if they had been drinking in the park. Of course they told me no.

"OK, someone here was drinking, so whoever was not drinking get up and leave the table now," I stated.

Everyone got up and left. I found a bag of beer under the table. I took it and dumped it in the trash and let dispatch know that the situation was taken care of. I got high marks for my quick thinking to defuse a potentially dangerous situation.

1920,Shots Fired, Officer Down. HPD Officer Stan Cook

On July 18, 1989, in the Pacific Ballroom of the Ilikai Hotel, thirty-eight of us took the Oath and became badged officers of the Honolulu Police Department. We called ourselves The 38 Special. I proudly wore badge number 2427.

Chapter 3 Police Rookie

AFTER GRADUATION THE FIRST

thing that happens is you must go through the FTO program. FTO means Field Training Office. In this program the new officer is assigned to a "seasoned" officer. That officer is called your FTO. He usually is a "motor" officer. Now I know that on the mainland a motor officer is a motorcycle police officer. In the Honolulu Police Department when you are a rookie you drive a white police cruiser. After you have around five years in the department and climb to the top of the "motor list" you are allowed to buy your own police vehicle. It can be most any car but has to be on the approved list of the department. It is a subsidized program.

1920,Shots Fired, Officer Down. HPD Officer Stan Cook

The police department covers your insurance basic maintenance and gas and oil that you use on the job. The department installs the radio, siren and flashing blue light. The blue light is on a strap that is clamped to the top of your vehicle when you are on duty and stowed in the trunk when you are not. In many cases this becomes your family car when you are off duty. As a police officer you need to carry lots of "stuff" such as books, report papers, a fingerprint kit, other weapons, a baton, a flashlight and, well, you get the idea. When you are a rookie you have to carry all that stuff in your personal vehicle and then as your watch begins you have to check out a white cruiser, drive to where you parked your personal vehicle, take the "stuff" out and put it in the trunk of your cruiser. After your shift you have to do the reverse. It is basically a pain in the ass. Once you have your motor all you have to do is strap the blue light on top and you are good to go. Yes, getting your motor is a big deal. The first thing a rookie riding with his FTO learns is to respect his motor.

Most police departments run on three shifts. 1st watch is like the graveyard shift, 2nd watch is the day watch and 3rd watch is the afternoon and evening watch. The day after our graduation I was ordered to report to the District One office and was assigned to FTO Officer Ross Fukuda. Most FTOs have a reputation as being hard asses and I guess that is as it should be. Ross, however, was really into the teaching part and that too is as it should be. I think my maturity and military background really helped a lot in seeing me through the FTO program. I had two other FTOs, as our days off would not always match. Each of the FTOs that I was assigned to taught me a lot. I

1920,Shots Fired, Officer Down. HPD Officer Stan Cook learned early to keep your ears open, work hard and go the extra mile. Above all, don't complain.

My first day on the road with Ross was a real eye opener. The academy was really great. I learned a lot and it prepared me well for what I would face however, I think no matter how much they teach you in the academy, nothing can really prepare you for the real deal. As soon as we checked in we were sent to a case. If I remember correctly it was a burglary of a dentist office, followed by a briefcase found on a sidewalk and then by a theft at a store. We would no sooner finish one case than we were called to another. The trick is that while you are on duty you have to write your reports and have them ready at the end of your watch. In those days, because they knew a new officer would find it hard to finish the reports, they would allow us an hour or two after our watch to finish. That was a good deal for the FTO since that counted as overtime. Once you were on your own you would be expected to have your reports ready for turning in at the end of your eight-hour shift.

The FTO program went well and I was passed on to the next phase of training called "The 4th watch." 4th watch would be the first time I was allowed to operate on my own and yet still be under the supervision of a sergeant. The 4th watch consisted of was walking a beat and carrying all the ticket books and forms you would need for the shift. Most of the time the 4th watch consisted of walking a beat in Waikiki at night or in downtown Honolulu. Most of our class, including me, was assigned to the Waikiki area.

It is about this time that we started talking about going

to the watches. Upon completion of 4th watch and probation, you would be assigned to a district and begin patrolling on your own in a police cruiser. Or you could be assigned to the receiving desk. WHAT? Yep, the receiving desk, which is really the jail and the place that the bad guys are brought in for booking. We learned early about the receiving desk. It was a place that nobody really wanted to be assigned to. After all we were working hard to make it out to the watches. There was really no way to figure out who would go there and who would not. There was a feeling though, that if you made a good statement while in 4th watch you might be spared that assignment. I think really good stats made the difference.

It was my idea to work really hard while in Waikiki. I decided to give at least a book of parking tickets every watch and as many moving tickets as I could even though I was on foot. After all, it was Waikiki and with all its traffic it was not that hard to run after a vehicle that made a moving violation. As it turned out I was number one in parking tickets and number two in moving violation tickets. I worked my cases that I was assigned to and always turned in my reports on time. The upshot of all of this I was not assigned to the receiving desk.

The only problem I had was the old hearing thing again. At the end of our 4th watch assignment, we also came to the end of our probation time and that meant another physical and another hearing test. Again I flunked the 3,000 Hz tone in the left ear. What the hell was I going to do now? I didn't want to come all this way and get fired for medical reasons. A week after the physical I got a notice from personnel that told me the same thing I was told way back in the beginning. Go find a private doctor and have your hearing tested again. I went to two of them but had the same results. Yes, I went back to Kaiser but the female doctor that had passed before was no longer working there. I was sunk. There was nothing else I could do so I told my 4th watch sergeant what was going on. He set up a meeting with the Waikiki Major Jerry Brown.

The following week I sat down with Major Brown and my Sergeant Epstein. I told Major Brown that I had tried to get an outside test. The up shot of all of this was what the major told me.

"Stan, read my lips. Get your hearing tested again!" he said.

I told him okay and that was the end of the meeting. I feared I was at the end of my short career as a Honolulu Police officer. I would just continue on doing my job and wait for the ax to fall.

About a week later I received an envelope from personnel. I knew this was it. My ticket home and back to civilian life. I slowly opened the envelope, pulled out the letter that stated I had passed my physical and had completed my probation. Are you kidding me? How the hell did that happen? It was not until years later, after I had retired, that I had an occasion to meet with Jerry Brown who had also retired.

"Tell me the truth Major. It was you that took care of my hearing problem wasn't it?"

"Yes, you were too good an officer to let go," he told me. That was all that was said. We shook hands and I have never seen him since.

A week later our class got assignments to the watches. I was assigned to District 7, East Honolulu, right where I lived and where I wanted to go. It was great but it lasted only a week. What happened was that there was a unit that worked in downtown Honolulu called the Downtown Task Force. A week before we were assigned to the watches the Chief had disbanded the Downtown Task Force. The mayor at the time, Frank Fasi, called the chief. He told him he wanted the Downtown Task Force reestablished. The officers that had been assigned to the Downtown Task Force were senior to us, so guess who was called back to start walking a beat again? It is not the nicest part of town.

We walked the beat with the Downtown Task Force for several weeks. We understood that we would have to work there until the next class left the 4th Watch. We were hoping against hope that we would return to District 7. Word on the street was, however, that officers were needed in Pearl City.

Not long after that, we got the word. Sure enough, we would be going to the watches in Pearl City. We thought for sure that after our efforts in downtown we would get to go back to District 7 but it was not to be. We packed our gear, emptied our lockers in the main station and headed for Pearl City Station. Wayne Kama used to tell us in the academy "Life's a bitch."

Pearl City was a big district and there was there was a

1920,Shots Fired, Officer Down. HPD Officer Stan Cook

lot to learn. At that time the whole of the Waianae Coast was included in Pearl City's District 3. Since we were all white car [5]drivers some of the time we were sent to Waianae to work out of the Waianae sub station. The Waianae coast included Waianae Town, Makaha, Maili and Nanakuli and was a bit rougher than the Pearl City area. It had a lot fewer streets to remember and was kind of a "wild west" place to work.

One thing I didn't like about working in Pearl City was some of the time we were assigned to work in the station to work as a RTO[6] (Radio Telephone Operator). It sounds like a radio operator job, but in reality it was a paper pusher job. You had to answer the phones, take cases that walked in the door, fingerprint and book prisoners, plus file reports. It was a real suck job. I hated it.

Then came a time when the powers that be decided that Waianae should have regular white car drivers assigned. The Pearl City major, Lee Donohue, met with us all one day to let us know what was going on. He was looking for volunteers to work out of the Waianae station.

"Do you have to work RTO out there?" I asked.

---

[5] A white car is what we call the normal police cruiser. In Hawaii, after serving about 5 years you are allowed to buy an approved private car that the department outfits with a radio, siren and blue light. You then use this car as your police car and your private vehicle. It is called a subsidized program.

[6] RTO means Radio Telephone Operator. In HPD substations it also means answering the phone, taking cases coming off the street, filing paper work and booking arrested people.

1920,Shots Fired, Officer Down. HPD Officer Stan Cook

"No RTO work but you will do your own bookings. It is a lot further for you to drive too. Something to think about." he said.

My good friend, Virgil Ford looked over at me. We both simultaneously raised our arms.

"OK, Cook and Ford. You are assigned to Waianae." He turned and walked out of the room.

Chapter 4 Working Towards Solo Bike

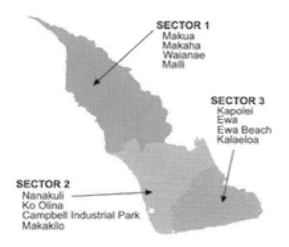

I WORKED IN WAIANAE for a couple of years. The longer I worked there the better I liked it. Granted, it was a long way to drive to get to work. It was on my own gas too. What made up the difference was that Waianae had its own courthouse. When I was supposed to go to court and was not on duty, I would get paid overtime and mileage from where I lived in Honolulu. Also, we were much more on our own out there and got to participate in many more interesting cases than we would have as a white car [3]driver in Pearl City.

I could write another book about working out there. Still, in my mind I never lost sight of my goal of getting into the traffic division and becoming a solo bike officer. So, how to go about it?

One thing I knew I had to do was to let the Traffic Section know who I am and that I wanted to be a solo bike officer. I needed to be the squeaky wheel. Since most officers must have five years in the department before they are considered, I had an up-hill climb.

My first step was to visit the Traffic Office in the main station, downtown, to visit with Lt. Al Lewis who was the LT for the Solo Bike detail. I wanted to try and find out what my chances were and to let him know my interest.

On my first visit to the Traffic Office I spoke with Lt. Lewis. I told him of my desire to be a Solo Bike officer. He asked me how long I had been in HPD and if I had a motorcycle license. I told him that had been in HPD for about 2 years and I did have a motorcycle license. Lt. Lewis informed me that they were trying to put together another solo bike class but there was nothing set yet. He took my name and said he would let me know if something changed.

1920,Shots Fired, Officer Down. HPD Officer Stan Cook

When I left Lt. Lewis's office I had a feeling that it was a nice visit but not much more than that. I decided I needed to do three things. First I made a promise to myself that I would visit Lt. Lewis once a month. That wooden chair is mine. Second, I would need to make friends with as many solo bike officers as I could. Since they spent a lot of time at the Waianae court, I could meet them there on days that I had court too. Third, I would concentrate on making all the traffic stops I could.

I felt so sure about the good results that would come from pushing traffic stops that I purchased my own radar gun. The reason I had to do that was because Waianae station only had three radar guns, which were almost always checked out by the senior officers. About the only time a junior officer would get a chance to use one of the radar guns was in the middle of the night after traffic was near nothing. So, buying my own radar gun would pay for its self. I later sold it to another officer. Incidentally, that officer used it to measure baseball speeds with his Little League team.

About six months later and several trips to visit Lt. Lewis's wooden chair, Sergeant Woodward, a solo bike sergeant, rode out to Waianae station to tell me that Traffic had decided to accept me in the next solo bike class. He said they would be contacting me.

Sadly, Solo Bike Officer Randal N. Young Born: September 19, 1945; Appointed: January 30, 1986 was killed: August 28, 1991 after being hit by a drunk driver while making a traffic stop at night on the Pali highway.

I did not know Randal personally but every time we

21

1920,Shots Fired, Officer Down. HPD Officer Stan Cook

lose an officer it is just like losing a family member. In fact he was a family member and it always hurts. Every time a solo bike officer is killed or badly hurt it brings up the question: do we really need solo bikes? The answer is always "yes" after an extended period evaluating solo bike use. The fact is that during periods of heavy morning and afternoon traffic nothing can get to an accident or other traffic tie up like a solo bike. Nothing can spend the time doing traffic control and catching traffic violators like a motorcycle. Nothing can escort the President and other heads of state like a solo bike officer. Is riding a motorcycle dangerous? Sure. But Officer Young was not killed because he was a solo bike officer. He was killed by a drunk driver while doing a traffic stop, the same type of traffic stop that he might have been doing if he were driving a police car. Nonetheless, the powers that be put a hold on any new solo bike class while the evaluations about solo bike started again.

OK, so I knew at this point that I would have to wait longer. At least, I figured, I was still in the running. Now I need to figure out a way to keep my name up front and on the list. Working in Waianae was okay but I needed to be closer to the main station, even working out of the main station. I put in a request to swap with someone that was working in District 7 and who wanted to work in Waianae. As it turned out I only had to wait a couple of weeks. I was contacted by personnel and told that an officer wanted to swap. I would start the following week in District 7. Perfect!

In mid 1992 I was assigned to "C" watch District 7, which is called East Honolulu. I continued to visit Lt.

1920,Shots Fired, Officer Down. HPD Officer Stan Cook

Lewis…to this day I don't know what he thought of my monthly visits.

During this time I decided to do a couple more things to keep my name out there. First, I decided to try out for the FTO (Field Training Officer) program. Here again I was working against the grain with really not enough time in the department. Most officers accepted into the FTO program had at least five years seniority and were already driving their own car. About that time I found out that Lt. Lewis taught a motorcycle safety course on the weekends. It was a course sponsored by the Motorcycle Safety Foundation and was open to anyone who had a motorcycle license and a motorcycle.

In the weeks that followed I filled out an application to be considered as a FTO and also applied for the motorcycle safety course. I was given a date for the next course.

After an interview with the FTO program, I was accepted and sent back to the academy for training to be a Field Training Officer. On the weekends I took the motorcycle safety course taught by Lt. Lewis. By taking this course I wanted Lt. Lewis to see that I was serious about riding and that I could ride. By passing this course I also got a good break on motorcycle insurance.

Upon completing the FTO program I was sent back to District 7 and started my duties as a Field Training Officer. Early in 1993 I was informed that I was to report to the Traffic Division for an interview. Solo Bike? Not yet. The word was that the Traffic Division was putting together a traffic enforcement section composed of black

1920,Shots Fired, Officer Down. HPD Officer Stan Cook
Chevrolet Camaros. It also turned out that almost everyone accepted to this division was on the list to become a solo bike officer. Finally, my foot was in the door.

We did some driver training at the academy and then hit the road early one morning. It was a real surprise to the public since they had never seen HPD black Camaros before. We were also using a very low profile light bar on top of the car, which was hard to see in the rear view mirror of the violator's car. This made it easier for us to pace speeders. It was good duty and as near to solo bike as you could get on four wheels. It was a happy time for all of us. We were having fun doing something new and different and being in the Traffic Division where we hoped we would be noticed.

After three or four months driving the Camaros they made a list of possible officers to be included in the next solo bike class. My name was on the list, but not many of the other Camaro drivers. Traffic Major Boisse Correa, Lt. Lewis and a couple of the solo bike sergeants interviewed me. [Major Correa later becomes Chief of HPD]. The only question I really remember was when Major Correa asked me what I would do if I stopped a car and the driver rolled up his widow and refused to talk to me. I told him I would call my sergeant.

"Ah see," he said. "This guy is going to put you to work. I like that." I was not sure at the time if that had been the best answer. It must have because within a week I was informed that I would be starting Solo Bike class.

24

Chapter 5 Solo Bike Training

SOLO BIKE TRAINING consisted of several weeks of intense training. The training areas included the parking lot of Aloha stadium, the motorcycle driver's license testing area at Kapiolani Blvd and King Street, the police academy EVOC[7] (Emergency Vehicle Operations Course) training course and on the road.

First we were outfitted with light blue overalls. Our name was attached on the right side pocket and a large patch on the back that said POLICE. On the left shoulder was the HPD patch and right below that was the somewhat smaller patch of the winged wheel, known everywhere as a symbol for traffic police officers.

The Harley Davidson FXRP motorcycles we used were

---

[7] EVOC is Emergency Vehicle Operation Course where police officer learn and practice emergency driving.

1920,Shots Fired, Officer Down. HPD Officer Stan Cook
stripped down. It was well known that during training
there would be many times that we would drop the bike,
so unneeded and easily damaged equipment was taken
off.

To start off the training we would go to the large
Aloha Stadium parking lot. Empty during the week, it
was ideal for a place to learn to ride and practice many
complicated maneuvers. We would meet at the police
station where we would drive a couple of police vehicles
to the stadium, while our instructors would ride some
training bikes. We were not yet trusted to ride the bikes to
the stadium.

Our instructors included Lt. Allan Lewis, lieutenant in
charge of the solo bike detail for the traffic division and
Officer John Veneri, one of the senior riders.

To be chosen for solo bike training you had to have a
Hawaii motorcycle license. Sometime officers were
selected with the agreement that they would get the
needed license within the early part of training. As I
remember we had one or two officers that needed the
license. The reason that this was not a problem was
because as part of our training we had to complete the
license course by riding it many times.

The license area was operated by the State Of Hawaii
and was located under the H-1 freeway at the intersection
of King and Kapiolani Blvd. There was an office and a
riding area laid out with orange traffic cones. The course
was very small and tight but we mastered it. Within a
couple of weeks our officers who did not have the
motorcycle license in the beginning, now had them.

1920,Shots Fired, Officer Down. HPD Officer Stan Cook

Many of the local riders (non-HPD) testing for their license would go to Waikiki and rent a moped type vehicle. They were allowed to take the test using this small, lightweight and easy to turn bike (of course we were not). It was fun to show up on a testing day and watch the local riders attempt the course using those small bikes. Only once in a while would someone show up with a larger bike and many times we saw him or her fail. The most fun was to watch their faces as we would then ride a large Harley Davidson through the course and never hit a cone. It was fun to watch our unlicensed officers go though the course with ease while the locals with their small bikes and mopeds, would have to work so hard to make it though.

Now that we had a little training, we were at a point where we could pick up the training bikes in the morning at the main station and ride them to the training area. We would either train at Aloha Stadium or the Academy in Waipahu. Some days we would just "pack ride," which was also an important part of training. Pack riding was done with the most senior rider at the front left position, the next senior to his right and so on to the end.

Nothing looks better than a pack of 8 to 10 bikes riding side-by-side and nearly wheel-to-wheel. We were told that if you can see the license plate of the bike in front of you, you are too far away.

This training was really important because we would always pack ride wherever we went. I remember one night, a year or two later, we were coming back from working nighttime traffic in Waianae. We were heading back to the station, eastbound on the airport viaduct,

27

1920,Shots Fired, Officer Down. HPD Officer Stan Cook wheel to wheel at 110 MPH. That gets your attention and is exhilarating!

Pack riding on the highway was fun, but we also did a lot of other things: riding up and down the very winding two-lane road on the side of Tantalus, riding from Schofield Barracks over Kolekole pass into the Waianae side and even riding on the windward side just to get the feel of riding in a stiff wind. The bottom line is you learned to trust the guy in front, behind and alongside of you.

Part of our training and by far the hardest, was riding in and out of traffic cones at Aloha stadium. To me the hardest was riding in the figure-eight cone pattern. To look at it you would swear that you could never turn your motorcycle in that small area. So, on our first try, Lt. Lewis and John Veneri both went into the figure eight to prove that it can be done. Then to top it off, they both went in at the same time with one on one side and the other on the other side and without meeting at the crossover. So, okay, it can be done. It was really a matter of leaning the bike so far to one side that the foot

28

1920,Shots Fired, Officer Down. HPD Officer Stan Cook
platforms would scrape on the asphalt, while at the same
time leaning your body hard the other way, while
maintaining just enough power to keep the bike from
falling over.

Why you ask? This was a skill that we would use a lot
in the future when riding through heavy traffic on the
freeways going to the site of an accident. I really
struggled with this exercise. In my mind I was afraid I
was not going to make it past this. I remember at one
point we were coming back from Hawaii Kai after riding
on the steep roads there. We were pack riding to Aloha
stadium to do more figure-eight riding. As we passed the
off-ramp to the main station, I was thinking I could take
the off-ramp and quit. I kept telling myself that going
back to patrol would not be that bad. We were coming up
on the off ramp and I was riding on the outside so it
would be easy just to peel off. "Here it comes" and we
rode right by it. I just could not do it. I had worked too
hard to get to this point. If I quit now I would never be
the same. It was just time to gut it out.

That afternoon I made it through the figure eight for
the first time. I was so excited when I came out of it I
gunned the engine and ran into a Jersey barrier. No
damage or injury but I remember looking at the wall and
seeing the black mark where the tire hit and you could
read the words Dunlap. Of course my buddies took a
picture of it and posted it in our lineup room in the traffic
office. I took some ribbing but I didn't care. I had done it.

The weeks went by and we got better, feeling more
comfortable doing the things we were going to have to do
once we were certified. We got so good at the figure eight

29

cones that we could put three bikes inside and ride. I say "we," but not me. I never got that good at it. The last part of the training was riding up Pele Street and making a U turn in the middle. This was a very steep road on the hillside by Punchbowl. It was one of the final tests that we dreaded but looked forward to at the same time.

Think about it. You have to ride up this real steep hill then make a U turn leaning into the hill and wind up coming down again. Let me put it another way: it was steep enough that if you fell over, your bike would start sliding down the road. Turns out we did fine and it was really a lot of fun.

The next challenge was to ride in loose dirt in a hilly area. This was done in a special area next to an old pineapple field. Now, these Harley Davidson bikes are not made for dirt bike riding. But if you know what you are doing it can be done. That was another good day. Not really a pass/fail kind of thing, just enough to give you knowledge of what to do in loose dirt. Keeping your motorcycle clean was also very important, with near-daily inspections. Most of use decided then and there that if a suspect ran into the dirt fields we would just call the helicopter or "1290" as its call sign was then.

The last big test was called the "slide for life" which we had been hearing about for a long time. The idea was that, back at Aloha stadium in a straight flat area, we would get the bike up to about 30 MPH and then lay it down, so that you learned how to survive that kind of fall. On the appointed day we were wearing our coveralls padding added here and there. We were to use a really stripped down training bike.

1920,Shots Fired, Officer Down. HPD Officer Stan Cook

Okay, here we go. John Veneri would do it first to show us how it was done. "Man," we were saying, "I sure don't want to screw myself up now, right here at the end of training."

John got on the bike and took a couple of test passes and asked the Lt. if the speed looked okay. Lt. Lewis told John to just go do it. John seemed really nervous and acted like he really didn't want to go. He reminded the Lt. of what happened the last time they did this. John headed down range, stopped and waved his hand. The Lt waved him on. Here he comes. He really looked like he was going too fast. Right when he was supposed to lay it down, he stopped. rode over to us and told us that they don't really do that. It was all a joke.

Sworn to secrecy about the "slide for life," we were then certified and graduated a couple of days later.

In the past each class was divided up among the other squads. This time the Lt decided to keep us together and assigned us to a senior sergeant. Though Sergeant Ricky Seminara was a hard ass it all worked out in the end.

Chapter 6 August 31, 1994

IT WAS QUIET IN the bedroom of our Hawaii Kai home at 4 o'clock in the morning. Most working people didn't have to get up this early, but since we are traffic cops we have to check in and hit the road before the 'going to work' traffic starts. Plus, this was the first day back to school. We called it the "back to school jam." The reason is that in Hawaii private schools are the norm. That means a lot more cars on the road delivering the kids to school in the family car.

I got out of bed gently so as not to wake Fe who did not need to get up this early. Later she would be part of the back to school jam. She would be driving from

1920,Shots Fired, Officer Down. HPD Officer Stan Cook
Hawaii Kai to downtown where she worked. I was
scheduled to work the H-1 freeway around Waipahu.

I went into the bathroom, cleaned up and headed
downstairs to my office where I kept my uniform. I
looked forward to the early morning ride to the station on
Beretania Street. Sometimes, on the way, I would meet
my Kalanianaole Highway partner, Damian Barr. He
lived near Kalanianaole highway about halfway between
Hawaii Kai and the station. We would just enjoy riding
side by side in the cool morning air that was Hawaii at
the end of August. I still think that he would sometimes
wait and listen for the sound of my Harley coming his
way. This morning, however, he was not there and I made
the ride by myself, still enjoying the peaceful ride and the
early morning smells of the fragrant plants that grew next
to the highway.

I pulled into the main police station parking lot and
stopped at the gas pumps. It was normal to fill up in the
morning or after your shift. Either way you would need at
least a full tank for a normal shift. In the just under 5
years that I was on the bikes, I racked up a little over
100,000 miles.

After the fuel stop, I parked my bike in our designated
area and proceeded to the squad room for roll call,
inspection and assignments for the day. We also had to be
ready for an inspection of our bikes. This usually meant
at least an hour of cleaning every day, at home, after the
shift. If it rained that day there would be even a little
more cleaning. Let's face it, riding in Hawaii for eight
hours you are almost sure to ride in some rain. Boot
dryers in the garage at home are a must.

1920,Shots Fired, Officer Down. HPD Officer Stan Cook

We would meet in the roll call room, sign in and turn in our subpoenas for up-coming court cases, check any other paperwork that needed our attention, then line up for inspection. After inspection we sat at the table and Sgt Seminara gave out our assignments for the day. As expected, I was to work the H-1 freeway in the area between Waikele and the H-1/H-2 merge.

This was the first day of school and I knew it would be a mess on the freeway and even the side streets. As most schools in Hawaii are private schools, the kids for the most part, are driven to school by a parent. This made for an automatic recipe for heavy traffic. We were not disappointed, I was right, but luckily there were few problems. In most cases we would just stay out of the way and monitor the situation. We would always be near an onramp so we could get on the freeway and quickly make it to any point of problem.

We were lucky on this morning with little troubles. Since nothing major happened I didn't see any of my partners. By 8:00AM the worst traffic is really over. Since we were about 15 miles from Honolulu the traffic would lighten up in my area first. We were going to be working the freeway in this area during the day so we had decided to meet at a local restaurant for breakfast. I was heading west on the freeway and took the Paiwa Street off ramp. I was hungry.

Chapter 7 The Incident

I TURNED LEFT at the stoplight at Paiwa Street and crossed under the freeway. I was in the right lane and coming up on a brand new traffic light at a cross street. As I approached the light, which was red, I noticed a blue and white vehicle in the left lane with an old Hawaiian plate and a new or current tax sticker. Now, what this meant to me was that this person most likely did not have a current registration or insurance and it usually meant they did not have a drivers license either. Along with the fraud use, it meant at least six tickets. In the early 90s this was a standard thing for us and they just kept coming. So I figured here was an easy six tickets to start off my day and before breakfast. I do have to admit that I was a bit of a ticket hound. Most guys would have

35

1920,Shots Fired, Officer Down. HPD Officer Stan Cook
just keep going to get that breakfast that was waiting less than a mile a way, but not me. I stopped next to the vehicle and called in to the open passenger side window for the driver to pull into my lane and make a right turn onto the side street.

As we turned onto the street I looked up at the street sign as I always did to make note of where I was. Paiwa is a very common and well-used street that everyone knows and as I turned I noticed the side street was named Hiapo St. As you turn onto Hiapo Street, there is a small bridge of about one hundred yards long, over a cane haul road. The driver stopped his vehicle to the right on the bridge leaving me enough room to pull in behind. I dismounted my bike and approached the vehicle on the driver's side. The driver appeared to be a local Polynesian male wearing denim shorts and no shirt. The vehicle was very messy inside.

"Let me see your driver's license, registration and insurance card, or whatever part of that you have," I said.

"Oh I don't have that with me but I do have driver's license Officer", he said.

"Okay, let me see some form of identification." He reached into his wallet and pulled out a HMSA card, which is a Hawaiian Medical Service Association ID card. The name on the card was Ione Sinopate. I asked him if that was his name and he said yes and then gave me his social security number after I asked for it. In Hawaii, at that time, the driver license number was your social security number. I told him to wait there and walked back to my bike to check with Dispatch. After checking with Dispatch I found that he did have an active driver's license. The vehicle, which was not currently registered, did belong to his estranged wife. Dispatch also informed me that he had been arrested the week before for beating up on his wife. Since he was cooperative, I decided to just give him a ticket for the no insurance. I wrote the ticket, went to the back of the vehicle and scraped the fraudulent sticker off the license plate. Since he was out of sight while I was scraping I had my left hand on the bumper to feel for movement. I felt a movement and popped up my head to see him moving around in the driver's seat. Nothing suspicious, but it did raise my level of awareness a little. I then returned to the driver to issue the ticket.

THE SHOOTING

As I returned to the driver side door, I told Sinopate that since he had been up and up with me, I was only going to give him a ticket for the no insurance and let the rest go. He thanked me and then I told him that he was going to have to sign the ticket.

As I was about to hand him the ticket book to sign, I noticed a blue jacket on the front passenger seat. Just under the left front corner of the jacket I noticed something that looked like what we know as gunmetal blue. I was not sure what it might be; a gun, toy, radio, or something else similar to that? I didn't know, but I needed to find out. I asked him if I could see what was under the jacket.

"Oh, it is nothing Officer." As he said that, he reached for the corner of the jacket and tried to cover up the part that was showing. As he did that, the barrel, which was pointing at the passenger side door, was hooked onto the jacket so when he pulled on the jacket it just lifted the middle. There in full view was an AK-47 with a magazine in place. I drew my 9MM Smith and Wesson with my right hand while throwing the ticket book on top of the car. I pointed it right at his head.

"Don't touch the gun! Don't touch the gun!" I shouted.

He reached over and under the jacket and picked up the AK- 47 by the center stock with his right hand. Held it up and looked at me.

"But Officer, it's not loaded," he said in a semi-soft voice. He was holding the weapon somewhat close to the steering wheel. In a flash I thought that maybe I could reach in and snatch the weapon just like you would snatch a toy from a kid. I reached in with my left hand and grabbed at the stock. He then put his foot against the door, put his left hand on the weapon and pulled it out of my hand. I instantly realized I was in trouble and he now had complete control of the weapon.

"No more nice guy," I thought.

I turned quickly to my right and ran to the right rear of the vehicle and looked in the rear window while pointing my 9MM at him. I could see that he had the weapon's barrel pointing through the window with his finger on the

38

trigger and the barrel moving from right to left in my direction.

BANG! BANG! I fired twice at him even before I could consciously think about it. I have been asked several times since then about what it was or when it was that I decided to fire. My answer has always been that I never made a decision to fire. My first thought was, "Shit, I fired".

As I shot through the back window I knew that I hit him but however the back window spider-webbed from the gunshots and I, therefore, lost sight of the driver.

At this point I have no memory of what happened next. I surmise that he also shot through the back window and hit me at least once. We later found four holes through the back window. This "black out" lasted no more that 5 seconds.

The next thing I know I am lying in the street about 20 feet to the left rear of his vehicle. He is leaning out the driver side window up to his waist holding the AK-47 with the folded stock, in his right hand. He was firing rapidly in all directions. I was firing back at him as fast as I could. I could see blood flying, I knew I was getting good hits to center mass, but he just kept shooting.

I fired sixteen rounds, which was my magazine plus one in the chamber. I could now see that my slide was locked back indicating I was out of ammo. He appeared to be out of ammo also and looked like he was trying to reload. I dropped my magazine, grabbed another from my belt, inserted into my weapon, dropped the slide and

1920,Shots Fired, Officer Down. HPD Officer Stan Cook
aimed. During this shot time it gave me time to realize
that my hits to his center mass, as we are taught, were not
doing much good. As I resumed firing I aimed for his
head. I fired and I could see his head whip back. He kept
working on his weapon. I fired again to the head.

His head again whipped back but this time he dropped
the AK-47 and he hung out the window with his hands
hanging straight down. He was no longer moving.

I knew I had been hit but not how bad at this point.
The pain had not started yet. I crawled back to my bike
on my hands and knees. I placed my 9MM under my bike
for semi-safekeeping. I didn't know if or when I might
pass out. I grabbed the microphone and called out; "1920,
shots fired. Officer down!"

Dispatch: "Unit?"

"1920. I've been hit!" I said.

Now the radio traffic went crazy. Dispatch asking where I was. Other police units were trying to get information to come and help me.

Dispatch: "1920. What is your location?'

"Suspect's dead." I called that off quickly to make sure the units coming to help knew that there was no threat. I just need medical help. I just could not remember the name of the main street. I knew I was on Hiapo Street. Hiapo is a small side street off of the main street named Paiwa. It has always been my policy to check the names on the street signs whenever I made a turn onto a new street. So why then could I not remember the name Paiwa? Well, later, when looking at the crime scene photos I noticed the street sign for Paiwa Street was missing.

Now the radio traffic was getting crazy. I could not get

a word in so I dropped the microphone. The pain was really setting in. I looked across the street and saw a female there in hospital scrubs. BUT she had a camera in her hand and she was taking pictures!

I yelled across the street to her: "Are you a nurse?" "Yes." she replied.

"Well put your fucking camera down and get over here to help me!"

This was Carlotta Ader who it turns out later was not really a nurse but worked in a local hospital as a tech. The Honolulu PD Detectives confiscated her film. She did have great pictures with the first one taken just as I was calling on the radio.

About the same time a local male ran over to help. He propped me up and held me in his grasp. Both the nurse and the male were there now doing what they could, which was not that much at this point.

Local residents began showing up. One male, a former University of Hawaii football player, ran over to the dead driver and kicked the AK47 from under his hands. It was a very smart and brave move though he was messing up my crime scene. I yelled at everybody to get out of the street and stay on the sidewalk. Again, training. Even in my condition I knew it would be important to preserve the crime scene.

Now, police units were arriving on the scene. One of my motorcycle partners, Michael Rapisura, arrived and came to my side. I gabbed his leg.

"It hurts Rap, it hurts," I said.

"I know Stan," he said, "the ten ten [4](ambulance) is on the way."

Rap stayed next to me all the way going into the ambulance. Sadly, as I write these words, I just found out that Michael Rapisura, HPD retired, passed away on this day, April 1, 2010, of cancer. He was a good man, great cop and a wonderful partner. He was there for me in my hour of need. God Bless you Rap.

1920,Shots Fired, Officer Down. HPD Officer Stan Cook

One of those helping me took off my helmet and boots. That picture wound up in the newspaper and almost become a symbol of what happened here.

The EMTs came to me. One male and one female, (names here Norman and Donna)

"What happened officer?" Norman said. "The guy shot me," I replied.

"How old are you?" "Fifty four." I replied.

"Okay, we're going to take care of you," Norman said.

They loaded me on the gurney, rolled me to the open door of the City and County of Honolulu ambulance and loaded me inside. The female started driving while Norman began tending to me. First he tried to remove my gun belt but was having trouble. I reached down and took it off for him. Then he started removing some of my uniform.

1920,Shots Fired, Officer Down. HPD Officer Stan Cook

I knew we were heading for Queens Hospital, the trauma hospital at that time. I remember how rough the ambulance rode. I mentioned it to Norman and he told me he knows they are rough riding. I had seen ambulances many times and had put hurt people inside them many times but had no idea how rough they rode. Damn, I was hurting badly now.

"Don't worry, we will get there quick. Traffic is opening right up for us," Norman said.

Later I learned that this incident was all over the morning radio. Officers were coming to help from all over the island. People were calling in and asking what was going on. The radio guys were telling the morning drive people that an officer had been shot and to just get out of the way. They were.

I could see out a window of the ambulance and as I know the freeway very well, I knew the overpasses that we were passing and was keeping track of our progress to Queens Hospital. I found out later that several fellow Solo Bike officers were escorting us.

Minutes later we pulled into the Queen's ER parking area and the doors were opening. My uniform had been cut open by this time but I pulled the part of my shirt that held my badge back to my chest. The next thing I saw was the Chief of Police, Michael Nakamura, standing next to me. He, of course, looked very worried. The only thing I could think of to say was:

"We won Chief, we won." I said.

1920,Shots Fired, Officer Down. HPD Officer Stan Cook

He said something to me but I don't remember what. Later he was interviewed by a TV news reporter and was asked if he got to talk to me before I went into surgery. He told her yes. She asked him what I said. He looked at the reporter sheepishly and said: "I don't remember." He knew but it was not to be reported to the press.

Michael Nakamura
HONOLULU POLICE CHIEF

During this time my wife, Fe, was at work. At her work place they always listened to the morning radio station K-59 with Michael W. Perry and Larry Price. They had already coined the term of Robocop for me. Of course at this time my name had not been released but somehow Fe knew something was not right.

She cleared her desk and waited for the phone to ring. She hoped it would be me letting her know that I was fine but when the phone rang it was Chaplin 1, Sister Roberta Derby.

She answered the phone and heard, "Mrs. Cook?" "How bad is he hurt?" she said.

1920,Shots Fired, Officer Down. HPD Officer Stan Cook

"He is alive and on his way to Queens. We have an officer on his way to pick you up and take you there." She said. "How did you know?" she continued, "Nobody was suppose to release his name."

"No" Fe replied, "I just knew".

An officer in plain clothes from CID (I forget his name and- wish I could remember) picked her up and went blazing down Beretania Street with siren only, not having taken time to install his flashing blue light. I was already inside Queens and getting ready to enter the operating room when Fe appeared at my side.

She had tears in her eyes and said: "You are going to be okay. Don't you leave me."

As they wheeled me into the operating room, I looked up at the guy at my head. "Who are you?" I asked.

"I am your anesthesiologist," he said.

"Okay, you are in charge of recovering the bullets," I ordered. Like they would really follow my orders. I guess it was just my inclination to stay in charge of what was going on.

The next thing I knew they were shoving a catheter in my penis, a finger up my ass and a tube going down my throat. At this time I knew I no longer had control and it was time to let them do their thing. Like I had a choice. I saw the anesthesiologist had a mask in his hand. I reached up, grabbed it and put it over my own mouth and nose and took a deep breath. That was my last act of control.

1920,Shots Fired, Officer Down. HPD Officer Stan Cook
    Lights out.

Chapter 8 The Aftermath

SLOWLY THE LIGHT CAME on. The eyes opened a bit and the memory came back a bit. I don't even remember the recovery room but I was now, I was told, in the ICU. I don't remember lot of the first few hours there. What I did remember most was that my mouth was dry and the nurse brought me ice chips in a cup. Let me tell you, ice chips never tasted so good.

There is a funny thing about my heart. Since I was 21 years old I had experienced an occasional skipping beat of my heart. The first time it happened was when I was out of the Navy for a year and working at Boeing in Seattle. I was at my workbench and all of the sudden my heart skipped a beat. It surprised me and scared me at the same time. I jumped up and started running for the medical care station that was not far away.

"I'm having a heart attack!" I was yelling. I ran into the medical station and the person there laid me down and took my blood pressure. Normal. Listened to my heart. Sounded normal.

"Let's do an EKG," she said. So, they snapped all the little buttons with wires all over my body and started the machine. She ran the test and after it was finished she informed me that the test was absolutely normal.

That began an experience that would follow me all of my life until this day in ICU. I often had this skipping of my heart, over and over again but every time I would complain about it to a medical person they would do tests and find nothing wrong or unusual. As I got older, the skipping became more frequent. Finally, having always passed my physicals, I gave up worrying about it.

As I was lying there in ICU with nurses in and out taking great care of me, one of the nurses looked up at the monitor screen.

"Oh, your heart does funny things." she said.

"You see it? Really see it?" I asked.

She told me she did and that it was nothing to worry about. I tried to tell her my story of feeling it all these years but she acted like it was really nothing. Well, at least somebody had seen it. It was not until years later and doing some research on Google that I found out what I have. It is called PVCs. Here is what I found out.

"Among the many different types of irregular heart beats, few have created as much consternation and confusion among both doctors and patients as premature ventricular complexes (PVCs). In various doctors' offices and at various points in history, PVCs have been regarded as either harbingers of impending death, or as completely benign phenomena that require no attention whatsoever."

Turns out it is a misfiring of the heart muscle. It is kind of like a timer that gets out of kilter. It does not really skip a beat. It fires a beat too soon and then there is a gap between that beat and the regularly scheduled beat. There really is nothing to worry about. The main thing that can aggravate it is a little too much potassium in the body. So I have learned to live with it to this day.

I do remember some officers coming in my ICU room that night but I really don't remember whom. I know Fe was there with me and that gave me great comfort. I do remember very strongly my need to tell my story. I had no idea at this point that all the TV stations in town were running stories and video of the incident. I don't recall the TV being on in my room or seeing any part of the TV news shows. I just needed to tell someone what happened.

Later that night Honolulu Mayor Jeremy Harris stopped by my room and apologized for not having come sooner. He asked me, "What happened?"

Oh my God, that opened the floodgates and out came my story from beginning to end. It was the first of many times I was to tell this story. As it turned out later when I saw all the newscasts that one of my daughters, Maya, had recorded for me, most people had it wrong. The HPD spokesman had it mostly wrong because he had not talked to me. Mayor Harris, on the other hand, told the story to the TV people the next morning and he had it right.

I don't remember how long I spent in the ICU. I was told that I had been hit eight times with .223 rounds from his AK47, the same round that our US Military M-16s and AR-15s use. Those eight rounds had made eleven wounds, because some of the rounds went in and came out. The medical term I was to learn was a fistula. I was hit on my right side and left side. My gun belt and holster tempered the right side wounds. I was hit on my right

1920,Shots Fired, Officer Down. HPD Officer Stan Cook
upper rib cage, a small wound on my face and a crease on top of my right forearm. It was later determined that this round passed by my right ear just missing my head. The rounds that I took up my rear end did most of the damage. Since I had been knocked to the ground, my legs and butt were directly in Sinopate's line of fire. Some of his rounds glanced off the pavement and went into my body through my read end. Somehow they all missed the Sphincter valve, which was a good thing.

The rounds entering my body did massive damage to my intestines and colon. The surgeons had to remove about ten feet. Still, I was lucky.

It turns out that I hit him with fifteen out of eighteen shots. There were twelve shots to the body and three in the head. Two of the three shots to the head were intentional. Those were the last two shots I made to end the shooting. I was amazed that during my first sixteen shots, one had hit in the head but, I guess, due to the Crystal Meth he was on, he just kept going.

I was told later that there was some chatter on the CB radios out in Waianae about getting the cop that took out their friend. Thus I had an officer at my door at all times and later parked in front of my house when I was convalescing. I don't really remember how long I was in the ICU. Seems to me it was three days or so, maybe less.

Anyway, at one point it was time to move me into a regular hospital room. The day I was to be moved several Solo Bike officers turned up. One of them was John Veneri. He really took charge. John went to the wing and floor where I was going and checked out my room. He

1920,Shots Fired, Officer Down. HPD Officer Stan Cook didn't like it.

"Too close to the elevator." He said.

So he walked down the hall until he found an empty room that he liked. "We will put him in here," he told the nurses. He then came back to the ICU room and told everybody that we were ready to roll. The people in charge of moving me to my new room got everything ready and opened the door. They pushed my bed down the hall with John leading the way, his hand on his gun. When we go to the elevator he went in first to check it out. We then entered the elevator and headed up to the floor I was to be on. When the elevator stopped John told everyone to wait. The door opened and John, hand on his gun, checked both side of the open door and down the hall. When it was clear to his satisfaction he looked back and gave the people waiting in the elevator a wave to continue. Once again when we got to the room John checked the room, the closet and the bathroom before he would let them wheel me in. I tell you one thing; John was not going to let anything happen on his watch. A few years later he would receive the Gold medal of Valor for a shooting incident near Koko Head.

I guess up to this time visitors were very limited. After I was moved into my own room I was amazed at what happened next. I had no idea that the newscasts of all the major TV stations in town carried something about my shooting every night and morning. I received hundreds of cards and letters.

1920,Shots Fired, Officer Down. HPD Officer Stan Cook

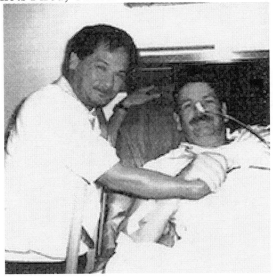

There were flowers everywhere. School kids made me banners. There were lots of food and cases of soda. All, of course I could not eat or drink, but the thoughts behind it all were amazing. At least the HPD officer stationed just outside my door got to eat well.

Some of the writings in the cards brought tears to my eyes. I received one card from a Japanese citizen that had been vacationing in Hawaii. On his way home, in a taxi going to the airport, he stopped at the hospital and dropped off a card for me. Inside the card were four crisp one hundred dollar bills.

Officer Danny Gooch brought by the first pictures from the scene. He had enlarged the photos to full size, so for the first time I saw the scene where it had all happened. At about this point I was really beginning to understand all that had happened. During a quiet time when there was only my wife with me, I was reading a card from a lady who had really been touched by it all. As I was reading the card out loud my voice began to quiver. Fe went to the door leading to the hall, closed it and came and stood next to me. That was when I lost it. I cried like a baby for several minutes.

My doctors were Dr Alan Cheung and Dr. Saito. I don't remember Dr. Saito's first name. I called him doctor pain. Why? Because every time he would check my wound he would stick his finger inside and make sure the outside of the wound was not healing faster than the inside. In other words they had to heal from the inside out. All I know is that it hurt like hell and I hated to see him coming in the door. I was not unhappy when several days later he was transferred to another hospital. He did tell me, however, that it was lucky that I was not wearing a bulletproof vest. He said he got his training in south central LA. He learned that when a .223 round goes in a vest it comes out the other side bigger than when it went in. This causes much more damage to the body than without the vest. Police officers are normally supplied with bulletproof vests designed to stop a bullet from their own gun caliber. In my case it was a 9MM.

By this time I had told my story to anyone that would listen. One day shortly after I was transferred to my own room, one of HPD's assistant chiefs came to visit me. "How are you doing?" he asked.

I told him how I was doing and started to tell him my story. "Oh Stan, stop. Has IA talked to you yet?" he said.

I told him that lots of people have come and gone and I don't now if IA (Internal Affairs) had stopped by or not.

1920,Shots Fired, Officer Down. HPD Officer Stan Cook
He told me that I should not be talking until I hear from
IA. He then left.

That is strange I thought. I have been here several
days and nobody had come by in an "official" capacity.

Later that day I got a phone call from a Lt. from IA.
He just had one question. He asked me where the Black
Talon bullet I had in my gun came from. I told him that
several days ago I and another officer had gone to Sports
Authority to buy some Black Talon 9MM ammunition.
When we got there they were totally sold out. The next
day during our line up I was complaining about the
inability to buy Black Talon ammo.

Officer Gary Mata was sitting next to me. He took out
one of his magazines of 9MM ammo, stripped off one
Black Talon from the top and handed it to me.

"I would hate to see you in a situation where you
needed one of these," he told me.

I thanked him, took the magazine out of my Smith and
Wesson 5906 and stripped of the top standard issue
9MM, gave it to Gary and put the Black Talon on top and
replaced the magazine in my weapon. Since we carry one
round in the chamber, the Black Talon would be the
second round out when I fired the weapon.

Here is information about the Black Talon from
*Wikipedia: "The Black Talon bullet is a jacketed hollow-
point bullet with perforations designed to expand sharp
edges upon impact.[1] The bullet included a Lubalox
coating, a proprietary oxide process, [2] (though widely*

1920,Shots Fired, Officer Down. HPD Officer Stan Cook

misreported to be Teflon, molybdenum disulfide, or wax) giving it an unusual black appearance compared to copper- jacketed or lead bullets. The Lubalox coating was to protect the barrel rifling and did not give the bullet armor-piercing capabilities. This coating in fact is still widely used on many of Winchester's rifle bullets today.[3] The bullet also had a unique appearance with a star shaped perforation on the black tip, giving it the nick- name.Winchester bowed to pressure and in 1993 removed the ammunition from public sale for a time and eventually law enforcement also bowed to the pressure, but at no time was it, nor is it presently, illegal to possess the Black Talon ammunition."

The Lt. told me that the Black Talon ammo was not authorized for HPD use. I told him that we were told it was authorized and that most of the officers were carrying that round. He then told me to not say anything and they would get back to me.

Great, I thought. The one thing that could screw up my case was the one thing that may have saved my life. As it turns out, the Black Talon was the second shot that I fired. My first two shots went through the back window, through the driver seat and into his back hitting his lower spine. In pictures from the morgue and from bullet fragments recovered from the body, it was plain to see that the Black Talon did its job. The suspect was paralyzed from the waist down and unable to exit the car and finish me off. Later that afternoon I got a call from IA stating that they were sorry and that they had found out that the Black Talon round had been authorized. They said they would come by the next day to take my

1920,Shots Fired, Officer Down. HPD Officer Stan Cook statement.

The next day, after my morning liquid breakfast, two IA officers arrived. They asked everyone in the room to leave and then closed the door. They had a tape recorder and told me they wanted to take my statement. They also told me that I could have a union representative present if I wanted one. I suppose I should have asked for one but I didn't and told them I had nothing to hide.

So I heard the same questions I had heard for several days already.

"So," one of them asked, "what happened?"

I just started in with my story once again. They ran the tape recorder and took notes and that was it. After the official business was done they warmed up a bit and exchanged pleasantries with me.

I guess my hospital guard duty was good. Every watch assigned an officer to sit outside my door and guard the room. Normally he would have been on patrol duty. During the daytime hours it would be an officer from the Traffic Division of HPD. Other hours an officer was assigned from the district that Queen's hospital was in, D-1. This was a normal assignment when we had a prisoner in the hospital or other situation such as mine where they wanted to make sure the press would not make it to the room. Also, I found out later, that there was still talk on the CB radios in the Waianae area that they would like to take care of the officer that killed their friend. You never know when that kind of talk is just talk or serious. Either way you can't take a chance.

1920,Shots Fired, Officer Down. HPD Officer Stan Cook

I was on liquids only. I met a new lady about this time. She worked for the hospital and had the duty of teaching and showing how to care for a colostomy. During my surgery they had to remove about ten feet of my intestines and colon. Plus there were several areas of cuts to the intestine that had been sewn up. Since they needed time for these to heal they had cut the lower half of my colon in half, made a cut in the stomach wall and stitched the exposed ends facing out.

The top hole was now covered with a colostomy bag and the lower hole was covered with a dressing. Her job and I don't remember her name, was to teach me how to use the colostomy bag during the healing process. Of course at the time and I guess even to this day, I call her the Colostomy lady. I remember sometime much later I met her in the Hawaii Kai Safeway. We were back by the meat area and we noticed each other. I felt kind of awkward at the time standing there, making small talk with her. However, she was a very nice lady.

While in the hospital she showed me how to change the bag and the sticky kind of donut device that stuck to my stomach where the plastic colostomy bag would snap on. She said that I was lucky over all. Had the bullets hit a more sensitive area I would have to wear the bag for life. As it was I would only have to wear the bag for a couple of month until my inside healed and then there would be another surgery they called a "Colostomy Take Down." Oh joy. I was not looking forward to another surgical stay in Queens's hospital.

Finally I was allowed to go home to continue healing. The hospital had done all they could do. I would be

1920, Shots Fired, Officer Down. HPD Officer Stan Cook assigned a home nurse who would visit me everyday. He would clean, check and redress my wounds. He was a young Filipino male that lived not far from my home.

Also during this time HPD officers guarded my home. During the day it was by members of the traffic section motorcycle officers. It was really good duty for them since they didn't have to work the highway, plus Fe is a good cook and kept them well fed. After hours one of the regular patrol officers would be stationed in his car in front of the house. They were well fed too.

A hospital type bed was ordered for me and placed in the downstairs living room. It was much easier that way since the master bedroom was on the second floor and walking was still a bit of a chore. That bed consisted of a frame, mattress, pillow and my CAR-15 semi-automatic assault rifle and me. Why? Because of the talk in the Waianae area, on CB radio, that Sinopate's friends wanted to get the cop that killed their friend. To my knowledge nothing ever came of it, but you can't be too careful. Even months later, when I returned to work, friends warned me that CB chatter was still going on.

After two or three weeks, I was able to get around. My wounds had healed to the point that they didn't need any dressing. The nurse was released and the doctor told me to start walking as much as I could to get myself in shape for the surgery to come. It was now October 1994 and I was feeling much better. I would take my pickup truck down the hill to a flatter area in a nice residential zone in Hawaii Kai. I would park the truck and walk for at least 30 minutes every day. I even got to the point where I could jog, just a bit. That did not feel good in my gut so

1920,Shots Fired, Officer Down. HPD Officer Stan Cook
mostly I just walked and walked. Boy, what I would
have given for an iPod in those days.

Toward the end of October my daughter, who lives in
Tucson and works for American Airlines, called to
suggest that I come there for Halloween. She thought it
would be good for me to get away, relax and also give Fe
a little time away from all that was going on. Since I was
an American Airlines parent, I had special flying
privileges. I checked with my doctor and he told me to go
ahead. So, I packed a bag with clothing and medical
supplies and off I went. It was good to see my daughter
and her family. Her husband and I even managed to
make it to Phoenix to see a NASCAR race. She was right:
it was good to get away.

After returning to Honolulu it was more of the same,
getting ready for the next surgery to remove the
colostomy bag, sew my colon back together and start the
recovery process all over again. I went back to walking a
lot but this time I just walked in the hilly area where we
lived. I have to say I really did enjoy those walks. It was a
kind of secluded time when I could think about what had
been and what was to come. The date selected for the
"take down" surgery was the week before Thanksgiving.
So, right away I knew there would be no turkey for me
his year.

We arrived early at Queen's Hospital. Fe's brother-in-
law, Cecil Hunt, was with us. He is married to Fe's
second oldest sister, Zen. Cecil has been a godsend
through this whole thing. Always there for us and would
be again in the weeks and months to come. As Hawaii
regional warehouse supervisor for Southern Wine and

61

1920,Shots Fired, Officer Down. HPD Officer Stan Cook
Spirits he was busy, but always found time for his family.
An important part of the Samoans heritage.

I was taken to a small curtained room, much like an ER. I met with the anesthesiologist and was soon taken to the surgery. I was placed on the table that was stainless steel. They put a warm blanket over me and inserted an IV in my arm. I was told that the doctor was caught in traffic and would be late. I remember thinking; "See? Things are going to hell without me." Sure, but it was a fun thought while I lay there listening to soft music. After a few minutes they came in and told me the doctor was here and is getting ready. And, -- lights out.

Recovery Number Two Begins:

And again, slowly the lights come on. So, as groggy as I was, I slowly lifted up the sheet to look at my stomach. Yep, the staples were back. Doctor Cheung had cut on the same line but with a little different direction around my belly button. I could see that it would never look the same. There were two small bandages where my colon had been stitched to my abdomen wall. That meant, I knew, that the surgery had been a success.

Later that evening Doctor Cheung came in the room and told me that all went well, that I would be under the care of an intern until I went home and that he would see me in his office after that. I don't remember the name of the intern, but he was young, a bit chubby and very friendly. He told me he had followed my story and was happy that he was able to help me the rest of the way.

During my recovery time I spent a very short time in the ICU and then was soon moved into the same tower I

1920,Shots Fired, Officer Down. HPD Officer Stan Cook had been in for my first stay. Not the same room, but many of the same nurses.

This time was not as tense as before. It was a matter of healing on the inside where they had stitched my colon back together and the same long scar down my front and running from the Zyphoid process to by belt line. Unfortunately, just like before, I would not get any kind of solid food until I pass some gas.

During this stay President Clinton was in town and the HPD motorcycle detail was escorting him around the island. It was disappointing to miss out on that. Escorting the president meant two things: lots of overtime and some great high-speed riding on an empty freeway. One of our bikes did take a tumble on an off ramp, but the rider was not seriously injured.

Things seemed to be going much faster this time. They got me out of bed and walking right away. I had no hospital guard this time. Friends told me to be careful because there was still talk that they wanted to get the cop, although I was told that it didn't sound as serious as before.

I had a feeling that hospital wanted to get me out of there as Thanksgiving was rapidly approaching. They would often ask how I was feeling and I told them I was still hurting. Then would then tell me that I would be fine. Sure enough, the last working day before Thanksgiving they discharged me to finish recovery at home. All the staples were out of my incision and I was eating semi-solid food. I really didn't feel like leaving yet, but what the heck, that was one step closer to getting back on the bikes and back to work.

Everything seemed to be going good at home. By this time there was no more police guard in front of the house. I imagine that the district knew I was back in the hospital and I just didn't tell them when I came home. I sure didn't feel a need for it at this time and I still had the CAR15 loaded for bear.

Just after dark the first night home I suddenly got a hell of a pain in my belly. Nothing like I had felt before. I knew this was something I didn't want to deal with, so Fe put me in the car and back to Queens we went. I think it was the day before Thanksgiving and a lot of people were already off for the holiday. We went to the ER and they called my intern doctor who shipped me right back to a room in the tower. To this day I don't remember what they did but they got rid of the pain by the next morning and sent me home that evening, Thanksgiving Day.

So now I was just recovering. Doing a lot of walking and weekly visits to Doctor Cheung. I still had a little sore spot on the right side of my abdomen, about the place where my appendix had been removed about ten years before. On my first visit to Doctor Cheung's office I had three questions for him.

One, why it took three hours for my second surgery, to which he answered that since he was in there he just did some "nipping and tucking". Next was why I had this pain on my right side. He said it was probably just a "stitch" that would go away in time. (It never did and I had that pain for fourteen years and for some reason was cleared during a first Colonoscopy.) And my last

1920,Shots Fired, Officer Down. HPD Officer Stan Cook
question, of course, was how soon I could go back to
work. He told me it depended on how well my recovery
progressed. Maybe another month or two and I could go
back to work. He also told me that I could hurry it up by
doing lots of walking, which I did.

"Why are you in such a hurry to go back to work?" he
asked me.

I told him that the solo bike detail is just for five years
and the clock doesn't stop just because you are injured.
He smiled and told me he would see what he could do.

The weeks that followed were boring. I did my walks
everyday up on our hill in Hawaii Kai. I made my
appointments with the doctor and started doing some
woodworking at home. It passed the time but I was really
getting "antsy" to get back on the road. I did have a few
more hurdles to overcome however.

One of these hurdles was my amount of disability.
How badly was I hurt? How much would the state have to
pay me and even was I healed enough to come back to
work at all? WHAT?

Leaving HPD was not even in my thinking. It never
dawned on me that I might not be fit to continue with
police work. My God, I thought, what if that happened? I
was not vested with the department, having only a little
over 5 years. To think that I could be dismissed with a
handful of money and a thank you was disturbing to think
about. However, I did have an appointment coming up
that would determine that very thing.

I don't remember where I went neither for this appointment nor with whom. I just knew it was with a doctor who would determine the amount of body loss of movement based on a percentage. This doctor had me do all kinds of tests like squats, jumps, twits and so forth. It took the better part of an hour. After it was over I got dressed and met with the doctor in his office. What he told me was that if it was determined that if I have over 50% loss of movement the department would most likely medical me out. I asked him what my percentage was and he asked me how badly I wanted to remain in the department. I told him that I would be devastated if I was released due to medical reasons that I was only doing my job when I was shot and I wanted to continue with my career in HPD. He then told me that it was really up to him to decide what percentage of loss that I had, but that if I wanted to stay in, he would have to list me as no more than 50%. I am not sure of the exact percentage, but 50% is what I remember now. He even told me an estimate of how much money I would receive. To this day I don't remember how much, but I do remember that I was going to be able to go back to work. It just seemed to me that he had a lot of leeway for making a determination of my condition. I felt that if I had told him that I did not want to go back and do police work anymore, he had the power to make it happen. Strange?

I later received the Silver Medal of Valor in a ceremony in the courtyard of the main police station. The civilian gentleman who rushed to my aid at the shooting also received an award from the City and County of Honolulu.

1920,Shots Fired, Officer Down. HPD Officer Stan Cook

Much was said about why I didn't get the Gold Medal of Valor. Chief Nakamura told me much later that he made the decision to give me the Silver, although all submitted paper work was for Gold. He told me that his reason was that my situation was thrust upon me. Gold metals are awarded to officers who rush into harms way.

Case in point was Officer David Foumai. In February of 1992 David was watching TV with is family when shots were fired in the parking lot. He rushed out with gun in hand and took care of the situation.

That situation to rush into harms way made the difference and he was awarded the Gold Metal of Valor.

Chief Nakamura told me that was how he based his decision and if I felt there was a problem with it he just wanted me to know. I told him that I totally agreed with the decision that he made.

Chapter 9 Samoans And Their Culture

IN THIS CHAPTER I talk about the Samoan culture and family life. Why this man cannot be accused of "another Samoan hot head". Nothing could be further from the truth, in my opinion. I don't think that ethnicity can be blamed as an overall cause of a person doing a bad deed. There has to be another reason why this man went so far as to feel that murdering was the way out.

Many people mentioned to me that here was another hot head Samoan guy that had gone wrong. This always bothered me. I have never thought that what happened to me had anything to do with him being Samoan.

For those who do feel that way, please read below what I have taken off of the Internet. At the end of this I will give you my thoughts about him and how, as a cop, I feel

1920,Shots Fired, Officer Down. HPD Officer Stan Cook about the Samoan community.

From Google:

In Samoa the aiga (extended family) is all-important. Every village is composed of several aiga. The larger the aiga the more important it is and more power it can wield in village affairs. This leads to, what is a usually, healthy competition between aiga.

Samoan families are usually large; it is not unusual for there to be 12 or more children. Traditionally members of the family would work land that was allocated to them by the matai, but now it is increasingly common for families to encourage their children to work in Apia so they can earn a wage.

There are now more Samoans living outside of Samoa than in the islands themselves. Most of these send money

1920,Shots Fired, Officer Down. HPD Officer Stan Cook
back to the family on a regular basis.

*Fa'a Samoa, means the Samoan Way. This is an all
encompassing concept that dictates how Samoans are
meant to be- have. It refers to the obligations that a
Samoan owes their family, community and church and the
individuals sense of Samoan identity. The concept of
respect is also very important. You must always respect
you betters, this includes those older than you, matais,
ministers, politicians doctors and teachers. This
unquestioning demand for respect is taking its toll in
modern Samoa as the younger generation, which is
invariably better educated than its predecessors,
constantly finds itself trying to balance the demands of a
conservative Samoan society with its knowledge of the
world, increasingly gathered from overseas education
and experience. This has lead to one of the highest
suicide [http:// www.samoa.co.uk/suicide.html] rates in
the world.*

*Fa'a Samoa is also evident in the legal system which
is actually two separate systems, a western style system
administered by a police force and justice department
and a traditional system administered at a village level.
The two systems do occasionally come into conflict with
one another but generally things work smoothly enough.*

I have always respected the Samoan community, their
family traditions and their culture. As a cop I can say that
as a friend there is nobody I would rather have covering
my back than a Samoan. As an enemy you will never find
a more ferocious, never give up person. One of the
hardest calls a cop can make is to a family disturbance or
domestic problem. Samoans never feel that they need

1920,Shots Fired, Officer Down. HPD Officer Stan Cook
outside help. They handle these things in family and
family-to-family within the community. There for a
domestic call to a Samoan family is, or should be,
handled differently than other families. You, of course,
have to do your job but you have to take into account
their culture. You have done your job if you can leave
with them thinking they took care of the problem and
really didn't need your help at all. And many times they
really didn't need your help.

So, in my case it was more the Crystal Meth that was
talking and taking the action. This was a former, well-
respected kid from Waianae. He was on the football team.
Had a family with three kids and a really good job. By the
time I came in contact with him he had lost his job, left
his wife and family and was living in a car. If fact he had
been arrested the week before for Abuse of a Family
Member, a fact that dispatch did not share with me.

Normally the Samoan community would have taken
care of him. Maybe they dropped the ball somewhere
along the line. It appears that nobody tried to help him.
He did have an uncle that lived in Waianae and was vocal
on the TV news after the incident. His only family at this
time was drug dealers and the drug itself. I think at some
point, maybe when I saw the gun, he was the family and I
was an outsider. In his drugged out mind the only answer
to this situation was to kill the cop. The last words I heard
him say were: "—I'll kill your ass." He was on his own,
living in a car, high on drugs, carrying a loaded AK-47
and had over $5,000 street value of Crystal Meth on him.

So, I don't blame the Samoan community or this
Samoan man. I blame the Crystal Meth he was taking

71

1920,Shots Fired, Officer Down. HPD Officer Stan Cook and the drug trade that lives in our Island home..

Chapter 10 Hawaii, you will always have to come home.

AFTER 43 YEARS IN Hawaii I retired from service in 1999. I purchased some wonderful land in the State of Washington in the Pacific Northwest, where I was born and raised. So we have lived here for 12 years and found that while traveling and exploring the mainland has been great, the pull to return home to Hawaii is strong and we are making plans to return. Why is that? Well, first the old saying that you never can come home is true.

Returning to the place we were born and raised is a letdown because it is never the same as when you left. I had an occasion to return to the town of Beaverton, Oregon where I went to school for 12 years. While the town looked much the same, the people had changed. Nobody waved to me as I drove down the street. Of

1920,Shots Fired, Officer Down. HPD Officer Stan Cook course, what was I expecting?

So, why is it that you have to return to Hawaii? What is the pull that gnaws at my gut? Why do I keep Hawaii News Now on my Facebook account? Why do I tune into KSSK on my iPhone and still listen to Perry and Price in the morning? I was not born there but yet it really is home. Why is that you say? It's simple, but kind of long to explain. If you have served your country and live in Hawaii the Aina[8] starts to get into your soul. If you were married there and had children there you are becoming part of Hawaii. If you have served in a city or state government job to love and protect Hawaii, you are becoming Hawaii. If you have served in her National Guard and traveled the world representing Hawaii you are Hawaiian. If you have had your parents, one or both, live, love and die in Hawaii, your love for Hawaii becomes even deeper. When you find your family and friends are more extensive in Hawaii than any place else in the world, you are part of Hawaii; he part that can never be taken away from you no matter where you are.

At the writing of this book we still live on the mainland and are planning on returning to our beloved Hawaii. Should something happen to me before we get there I know that I will be buried in Hawaii and then my body will truly become part of the wonderful land that we know and love: Hawaii.

---

[8] Aina is the spirit, the sole, the land of Hawaii.

74

Epilogue - Lessons Learned

In this chapter I talk about some of the lessons that I learned looking back with 20/20 vision. Some of what I say here will be controversial and some is just common sense.

I faced an AK-47 shooting a .223 round while I was shooting a Smith and Wesson 9MM round. My thoughts follow.

1. There is no such thing as a routine traffic stop. I

75

1920,Shots Fired, Officer Down. HPD Officer Stan Cook

guess that is kind of true but I made hundreds of traffic stops that were nothing more than routine. The trouble is that you never know it is not a routine traffic stop until the shit hits the fan. Then, if you aren't ready for it, it is too late. I used to say that most traffic stops are routine but be ready, always, for it to turn into a non-routine stop in an instant. During my second year on patrol I was working in Waianae driving a white car. During a "routine" traffic stop I was covered off [9]by my sector Sergeant Rodney Goo. He told me to always assume there is a gun in the car. I may never see it, thus no reason for a search, but just assume there is one there and act accordingly. I really took that to heart, especially in Waianae.

2. You can do more than double tap. The term double tap comes from the action of drawing your weapon to fire and pulling the trigger twice instead of once. When we were in recruit school it was never really explained how many times you should pull the trigger. Mostly we were shooting at targets and slowly aiming and pulling the trigger once, then aiming again and pulling again. The discussion about how many times you should pull the trigger came up from time to time but only with my classmates or patrol partners.

It was never mentioned officially. What I remember coming out of these talks was that for sure don't just shoot once. Double tap means you shoot twice. Thus I started sinking that into my brain. When I was at the range to practice on my own, I would draw and double tap. Looking back on it now I was really doing myself a

---

[9] Covered off is a police word for back up

disservice. Sometimes, as in my shooting case, you should pull the trigger more than twice, or three times, or even four or five. When I ran to the back of that car I looked through the rear window. I saw that AK47 coming out the driver side window, I aimed and pulled the trigger ... twice.

3. My gun was too small. When I graduated from the academy we trained with and were issued a Smith and Wesson .38 Special. Because of some early shootings that seemed to leave the .38 Special lacking and partly because it was time, HPD brought out the Smith and Wesson 5906 9MM. I got mine because I was a Field Training Officer and it was felt, rightfully so, that I should carry the same weapon as the officer I was training.

For those of you that don't know, the 38 special pistol is a six shooter. It was a revolver that had six rounds in a chamber. Once you discharge all six rounds you have to open the cylinder and push a rod at the end of the cylinder to eject the spent rounds.

Next you have to take a speed loader [10]from your belt and drop in six new rounds. Close the cylinder and you are ready to go. This operation also has to be done with the weapon pointing towards the ground so the new rounds would fall into the cylinder by gravity. This is an operation that is difficult to near impossible to accomplish while lying on your back.

---

[10] A Speed Loader is a device that holds six bullets in a plastic device. It enables the shooter to load six bullets in one motion.

On the other hand, the 5906 is a semiautomatic that carries a magazine of 15 rounds and one in the chamber. So, you could fire 16 times, drop the magazine with the push of a button, grab another magazine from your duty belt, slide it in the bottom, click a button and the slide would fly forward inserting the first round on top of the magazine. And you are ready to go. It can take about the same time to do both, but when finished you wind up with 15 rounds ready to shoot instead of 6. It also does not need gravity to complete this operation.

The trouble with the 38 special is that, for the most part, you needed to be standing or kneeling to reload. It could be done from a prone position but with difficulty. Gravity plays an important part in reloading the 38. The cartridge eject rod works fine but to make sure, you need to have the back of the cylinder below level or pointing to the ground. This will ensure that all 6 spent cartridges fall out. Next, with the auto loader you need to have the cylinder pointing down so the next six rounds will fall in place.

With the 5906, each spent case is ejected as you fired. When the magazine is empty you only need to push a button and the magazine falls out. You don't need to think a lot about this because due to your natural way of firing the grip, where the magazine is housed is almost always pointing down. And to re-load you just shove the new magazine in the bottom of the grip, push another button and you are ready to go.

For a long time I have called the 9MM a peashooter. Many departments have agreed with my way of thinking and have moved on to the 40 Cal weapon. For me, I wish

1920,Shots Fired, Officer Down. HPD Officer Stan Cook
I had been carrying a 45 on that day in August 1994. I believe that had I been using a 45 Cal and did my auto response double tap it would have been over right there. The force of a 45 round would have stopped him right there. Plus the blast of a 45 would have blown out the rear window giving me a clear view of his movements. As it was the window just spider-webbed and thus obstructed my view of the suspect.

During the time before World War I and World War II the military adopted the 45 Cal 1911 by Springfield. They found that it was useful in close action since it would stop and knock backwards a charging enemy. Most small caliber rounds will enter the body, but in most cases would not stop the forward movement of a solder with a fixed bayonet who still could puncture you just from the momentum.

Of course I didn't face a guy with a fixed bayonet, but he was high on drugs. I fired the first 16 rounds making multiple hits and he was still going. During the time when I saw I was out of ammunition and reloading, my mind clicked that shooting center mass, as we were taught, was not working. The next two rounds I aimed right for the head and that did it. As stated earlier, out of the 18 rounds I fired there were 15 hits AND of the first 16, one of them entered his head.

Okay, what about shooting for the head. The basic rule we were taught was that the head is small and a moving target. You were much more likely to get hits when shooting for center mass.

Note here that my gun was too small. The 9MM

1920,Shots Fired, Officer Down. HPD Officer Stan Cook rounds were not doing the job. Even with a round to the head he was still operating. Yes, mostly because he was on drugs. But because of the massive power of the 45 Cal round, my fight I believe, would have been over much sooner with much less and maybe no, damage to me. It is always said that the crooks are better armed than the cops.

You think? AK 47 with a 20 round magazine of .223 cal up against a 9MM peashooter. It's not rocket science.

Many departments today, including LAPD, teach officers to take two the body and one to the head. That works for me.

4. You don't have to make every traffic stop. It is true; you really don't need to make every traffic violation that you come upon. Someone once ask me, while giving a speeding ticket; "So, are you making your quota?" I told him no. We don't have a quota. We can give all the tickets we want to.

So, here was my dilemma in this case. In the early 90s Hawaii had a license plate with the bust of King Kamehameha in the middle. All the plates on Oahu started with an A, B or C. Kauai started with a K, Maui country an M and the big island a H. Sometime around 1992 the state changed to a plate with a rainbow and the plates started with an E then an F and so on.

So, some people felt that instead of paying the license fee they would just steal the month and year sticker of someone else's plate and who would know. Well, I figured out early on that it was easy to find a violator by

1920,Shots Fired, Officer Down. HPD Officer Stan Cook
just looking for the old plate with a current sticker. You
see, in the very beginning the A plates were replaced
before the B and C plates. So, my nickname for the
violation was an Alpha plate. 90% of the time when you
made this type of stop it was good for six tags. Expired
license tag, expired safety check, fraud use of tax sticker,
fraud use of safety sticker, no insurance and most of the
time no driver's license. What bothered me most was that
these guys thought we were too stupid not to see what
was going on. So, maybe I took it a bit personal but I took
it on myself to take care of the problem. Sometimes I
would just sit under the Makakilo overpass and wait for
the cars coming out of the Waianae coast. Seems like I
never had to wait more than a few minutes.

So, by 1994 this practice was winding down. All the
A, B and C plates had been changed over to the rainbow
plates and most people figured out their plan was not
going to work anymore. So, on the morning of August 31,
1994 I had just finished working the "back to school jam"
on the free way in the Pearl City and Waipahu area. Some
of the other officers that were working that morning had
planned to meet at a local restaurant for breakfast. I took
the off ramp from H-1 freeway west bound to Paiwa
Street.

Turned left at the bottom and headed for Waipahu.
The first stoplight was at Hiapo St and there it was. An
alpha plate two cars back in the inside lane. I know I am
going to breakfast but how can I let this pass. I pulled up
and told him to take a right onto the bridge going over a
cane haul road.

5. Call off on all traffic stops. Now this one is my bad.

81

1920,Shots Fired, Officer Down. HPD Officer Stan Cook

We are taught from the beginning and I drilled it into my FTO rider, call off on every traffic stop. I even used to wait until my rider appeared that he didn't know where we were and asked him what street we are on. It is important for the dispatcher to know where you are when you are in contact with a vehicle that may have committed a traffic violation on even if you have arrived at a case you were sent to. So, why didn't I call off?

It goes to an almost unwritten rule with solo bikes. Because we usually mass in one district that has one dispatcher, calling off on every traffic stop can nearly overwhelm her/him. When we are working the freeway, shooting radar or laser we make traffic stops one after the other. The dispatcher is there to issue cases to the district patrolmen, know when they arrive or depart a case.

Solo bike could literally clog the frequency to the point that the dispatcher would have a hard time getting other work done. That is not fair to the dispatcher or the patrol officers. So, we seldom called off. In fact the other unwritten rule was that if we heard one of our solo bike officers call off on a traffic stop we know that he was not comfortable and we would fly to back him up. (I say him because solo bike is usually male, however, in my time in the department there were two female solo bike officers.)

So, what happened in my case? It was 8:30 in the morning in a residential area off the freeway. It was just another Alpha plate stop. Six tags and I am out of there on my way to breakfast. In this case the driver did have an active driver's license. It was not on him but I did check with dispatch to find out information on him and the car. Okay, so now I throw a little blame. I did call in

1920,Shots Fired, Officer Down. HPD Officer Stan Cook
to find out his information. The dispatcher did see that he
had been arrested last week for abuse. At this point she
should have asked me if I was off with this vehicle and
what was my location. She didn't, partly because it was a
lazy morning, partly because it was a solo bike officer
who seldom calls off and partly because she was new and
in training. Nonetheless it happened and the fault still lies
100% with me. She never returned to work after that day.

6. Wear a vest? At the time of my incident there was no
department policy on wearing a "bullet proof" vest. Many
officers wore them and purchased them out of their own
pocket. When I was in patrol duty I nearly always wore a
vest. I even had one made that looked like our shirt
uniform without the tails and sleeves. I would carry it in
the car and could easily put it on while on the way to a
call. The reason I didn't wear one all the time was
because it was really hot during the day in Hawaii. Since
there was no policy about them you were not breaking
any rule by not wearing one. It was even noted in the
news that Officer Cook was known to wear a vest but that
was from my patrol days. However about this time the
department was really starting to look at developing a
vest policy. The fact that I was not wearing a vest seemed
to spur on the decision to get the vest policy rolling. Even
before I came back to work the department was paying
half the cost of a vest. I understand that later and even up
to today they pay for the whole thing just like any other
equipment. I agree with that for sure. You just have to get
used to wearing them in the sun. Might help on weight
loss, you think? Now the strange part about this whole
wear the vest thing. It turns out that vests are mostly worn
to prevent an officer being shot with his own gun. I don't

know all the stats but from what I have heard there are more officers, nationwide, shot with their own gun than the gun of a bad guy. AND in my case, I came up against an AK47. A vest is not designed to stop a rifle round. At Queen Medical Center Doc Suzuki told me that it was fortunate that I was not wearing a vest. He told me that he had been a resident in South Central LA and had seen a lot of rifle wounds. He said that when a rifle bullet enters a vest it expands to twice the size and come out the other side bigger than a 45 Cal round and then enters the body and does much more damage than if it had not passed through a vest.

Still, in my opinion, an officer is much more likely to be shot with a pistol than a rifle. Therefore wearing a vest is a good policy. If what happened to me then could happen to me now, would I have lived? We will never know.

One last thought about the hearing issue. For the most part, in years past, it was understood that once you passed your probation physical you were "golden." Barring any major physical problems, you were passed through. This included hearing problems. Every year I had a physical and I always passed the hearing.

About 1997 or maybe 1998, the City and County of Honolulu hired a new medical examiner. Under his rule, he issued a strict compliance with all medical requirements. About six months before I was due to retire, during my last physical, I flunked the hearing test. I was told to go out in town and find an audiologist that could make me a hearing aid for that one ear. A hearing aid that would help me pass the hearing test. I did just

1920,Shots Fired, Officer Down. HPD Officer Stan Cook
that. It cost me $700. I wore it once for the test, which I
passed and never wore it again.

I want to say something about being part of a police
department. The brotherhood that exists between officers
in Law Enforcement is very special. It is something that
only other brother and sister officers can understand.

I spent 22 years in the military. I spent 14 months in
Vietnam, four, two-month patrols on an FBM submarine
where we were part of the deterrent that keep the Soviet
Union at bay. I spent countless days submerged off of
Russian cities like Petropavlovsk and Vladivostok
watching the Russian naval power. And yet what I
remember most is my time with HPD and working close
to some really fine officers. We trusted each other to have
our back. Together we worked and played hard. I just
don't think you get that in the military. Most of my
dreams are about my time as a Honolulu Police Officer. If
I had it to do all over again I would not change a thing.
Well, with the possible exception of that one traffic stop.

If you are ever lost, remember this:

The lip of the Big Dipper always points to the North Star.

Stan Cook

About the Author

Stan Cook was born in Ashland, Oregon on May 10th, 1940. After WWII the family moved from New York City, his father J. Morgan Cook's duty station, to Portland, Oregon and later to Beaverton, Oregon where he attended grade and high school. He graduated in June of 1958.

After high school he completed two years of required Navy service serving on the submarine USS Wahoo (SS565). After a year of college he rejoined the Navy where he served in three more submarines and at ComSubPac where he advanced to Chief Warrant Officer. As a Warrant Officer he served as 1St Lt. of the USS Grapple (ARS7), Armed Forces Courier service and 1st Lt. of the USS Tawakoni (ATF114). He left the service in December of 1975.

Stan then started and ran an electronics store in Aiea, Hi named DelComs Hawaii.

In 1979 he became a radio deejay working a various radio station in and around Honolulu. He also worked in Magnum

1920,Shots Fired, Officer Down. HPD Officer Stan Cook PI, Jake and the Fat Man and T.J Hooker. In 1984 he was the MC for the Miss Hawaii USA pageant.

After working a couple of years for the Foodland Corp he joined the Honolulu Police Department in 1989. During his time with HPD he also joined the Hawaii Army National Guard and completed his military service with 22 years total.

In 1999 he retired from the Honolulu Police Department and moved back to the Pacific Northwest where he resides at the writing of this book with plans to return to Hawaii sometime after 2012.

1920,Shots Fired, Officer Down. HPD Officer Stan Cook

Contact Information:

You may contact me at stan@hawaiicop.com

At this writing my various websites follow:
http://stancook.com
http://websitesbycook.com
http://theshooting.com
http://hawaiicop.com
http://about.me/stancook
https://www.facebook.com/stan.cook
Twitter @stancook

———————————————

17403162R00051

Made in the USA
Charleston, SC
09 February 2013

To:

_____

Message:

_____

_____

_____

_____

Date:

_____

Blessings for Graduates

© 2012 Christian Art Gifts, RSA
    Christian Art Gifts Inc., IL, USA

Images used under license from Shutterstock.com

Printed in China

ISBN 978-1-4321-0179-4

Blessings *for*
GRADUATES

"I know
the plans
I have for you," declares the LORD,
"plans to
prosper you
and not to harm you,
plans to give you *hope*
and a
future."

JEREMIAH 29:11

Celebrating Your Accomplishment........................... 7

Pursuing Your Dream... 25

Tools for Your Success... 45

Sound Advice for the Road Ahead........................ 61

Celebrating You, Graduate!.................................. 73

There is a
good reason
why they call these ceremonies
"commencement exercises."
Graduation is not the end;
it's the *beginning*.

ORRIN HATCH

Celebrating Your Accomplishment

*A longing fulfilled is
a tree of life.*

PROVERBS 13:12

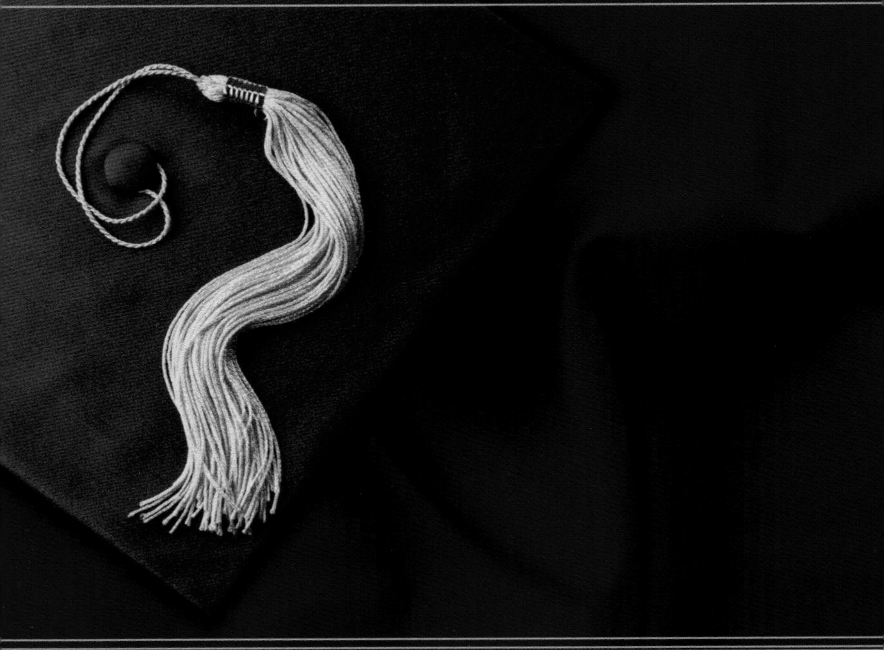

A Prayer for the Graduate

May you have enough *happiness*

to keep you sweet,

enough trials to keep you strong,

enough sorrow to keep you human,

enough *hope* to keep you happy,

enough failure to keep you humble,

enough *success* to keep you eager,

enough *friends* to give you comfort,

enough wealth to meet your needs,

enough *enthusiasm* to keep you

looking forward,

enough *faith* to banish depression,

and enough *determination* to make

each day better than yesterday.

ANONYMOUS

It is important

to recognize

that our

achievements

not only speak well for us,

they speak well for those persons

and forces,

seen, unseen,

and unnoticed,

that have been

active in our lives.

ANNE WILSON SCHAEF

"*Whoever* believes in Me,

as the Scripture has said,

streams of living water

will flow from within him."

John 7:38

High achievement

always takes place

in a framework of high

expectation.

JACK KINDER

The truth of the matter is that there's nothing you can't *accomplish* if:

~ You clearly decide what it is that you're absolutely *committed* to achieving.

~ You're willing to take *massive action.*

~ You notice what's *working* or not.

~ You continue to change your approach until you *achieve* what you want, using whatever life gives you along the way.

ANTHONY ROBBINS

You are educated.

Your certification is in your *degree.*

You may think of it as the ticket to

a *good life.* Let me ask you to think

of an alternative. Think of it as your

ticket to *change the world.*

TOM BROKAW

God is working in you,

giving you *the desire*

and the power to do

what pleases Him.

PHILIPPIANS 2:13 NLT

What *sculpture* is to a block of marble,

education is to the soul.

Joseph Addison

Great minds
have
purposes,
others have
wishes.
Little minds
are tamed and
subdued by misfortune;
but **great minds**
rise above them.

WASHINGTON IRVING

Believe
and
act
as if it were
impossible
to fail.

CHARLES F. KETTERING

The value of life

lies not in the

length of days,

but in the *use*

we make of them.

MICHEL DE MONTAIGNE

Dedicate some of your life *to others.*

Your *dedication* will not be a sacrifice;

It will be an *exhilarating* experience.

THOMAS DOOLEY

Your
greatness
is measured
by your **kindness.**
Your
education
and *intellect*
by your **modesty.**
Your real caliber
by the **consideration**
and **tolerance**
you have for others.

WILLIAM J. H. BOETCKER

The *Lord* grants
wisdom!
From His mouth come
knowledge
and
understanding.

PROVERBS 2:6 NLT

Sooner or later we all discover that

the *important moments* in life

are not the advertised ones –

not the *birthdays,*

the *graduations,* the *weddings,*

not the *great goals* achieved.

The real *milestones* are less prepossessing.

They come to the door of *memory*

unannounced, stray dogs that amble in,

sniff around a bit and simply *never leave.*

Our lives are *measured* by these.

Susan B. Anthony

Be wise

in the *way* you act;

make the *most* of every

opportunity.

COLOSSIANS 4:5

Pursuing Your Dream

*The desires of
the diligent are
fully satisfied.*

PROVERBS 13:4

The
mightiest
works have been
accomplished
by men who have kept
their *ability*
to dream
great dreams.

WALTER BOWIE

We can make our plans,

but the **LORD**

determines our steps.

PROVERBS 16:9 NLT

Dreamers see things in the
soft haze of a *spring day* or in the
red fire of a long *winter's evening.*
Some of us let these
great dreams die,
but others *nourish* and *protect* them;
nurse them through bad days till
they bring them to the **sunshine**
and **light** which comes always
to those who sincerely **hope**
that their *dreams* will
come true.

WOODROW WILSON

Keep your *heart*

open to *dreams.*

For as long as there's a *dream,*

there is *hope,*

and as long as there is *hope,*

there is *joy*

in *living.*

ANONYMOUS

May the LORD give you the

desire of your heart

and make all your

plans succeed.

PSALM 20:4

I hope your

dreams

take you

to the corners of your

smiles,

to the highest of your

hopes,

to the windows of your

opportunities,

and to the most special places

your **heart** has ever known.

ANONYMOUS

Dreams are renewable.

No matter what your age or condition,

there are still *untapped*

possibilities within you

and *new beauty* waiting to be born.

DALE TURNER

Most people never run far enough

on their *first wind* to find out

they've got a *second.*

Give your *dreams* all you've got

and you'll be *amazed* at the

energy that comes out of you.

WILLIAM JAMES

You can do what you want to do,

accomplish what you want to *accomplish,*

attain any *reasonable objective*

you may have in *mind.*

Not all of a sudden, perhaps,

not in one swift and sweeping act

of *achievement.*

But you can do it *gradually* –

day by day and play by play –

If you *want* to do it,

If you *will* to do it,

If you *work* to do it,

over a sufficiently long period of time.

WILLIAM E. HOLLER

34

Twenty years from now
you will be more disappointed
by the things you didn't do
than by the ones
you did.
So throw off the bowlines,
sail away from the safe harbor.
Catch the trade winds in your sails.

Explore. Dream. Discover.

MARK TWAIN

I don't think much of a man

who is not *wiser today*

than he was *yesterday.*

ABRAHAM LINCOLN

The *future* belongs to

those who *believe* in the

beauty of their dreams.

ELEANOR ROOSEVELT

Tune your ears

    to the world of

wisdom;

    set your heart

on a life of

understanding.

PROVERBS 2:2 THE MESSAGE

Use your head.

Make the most

of

every chance

you get.

EPHESIANS 5:16 THE MESSAGE

It seems to me we can never

give up *longing* and *wishing*

while we are *thoroughly alive.*

There are certain things we feel

to be *beautiful* and *good,*

and we

must hunger

after them.

GEORGE ELIOT

Cherish your **dreams**

and your **visions,**

as they are the children

of your **soul;**

the blueprints of your ultimate

achievements.

NAPOLEON HILL

You see things; and you say, "Why?"

But I *dream* things that never were;

and say, "Why not?"

GEORGE BERNARD SHAW

Success

isn't a result of

spontaneous combustion.

You must set

yourself on ***fire.***

ARNOLD H. GLASOW

Tools for Your Success

Wisdom brings success.

ECCLESIASTES 10:10 NKJV

Four Steps to Achievement

1. Plan purposefully

2. Prepare prayerfully

3. Proceed positively

4. Pursue persistently

WILLIAM A. WARD

Success means having the **courage,**

the **determination,**

and the **will**

to become the person you **believe**

you were **meant to be.**

GEORGE SHEEHAN

A Blueprint for Success

❖ *Know* yourself – *well.*

❖ *Prepare* a plan of action – but always have a *backup.*

❖ *Acknowledge* that there is more than one way to *achieve* your dream – maybe even two or three.

❖ *Own* your mistakes – and *learn* from them.

❖ *Recognize* distractions – before they *sink* your ship.

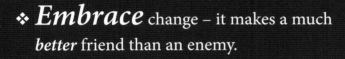

❖ *Embrace* change – it makes a much *better* friend than an enemy.

❖ Always *move forward* – nothing was ever *accomplished* by standing still.

❖ Accept the *reality* of calculated risk – nothing *ventured*, nothing *gained*.

❖ *Prepare* for a rainy day – *sooner or later* one will come.

❖ *Help* and *encourage* others along the way – you'll be a *better* person for it.

ANDREA GARNEY

No one ever attains very

eminent *success*

by simply doing what is required of him;

it is the *amount* and *excellence*

of what is over and above

the required that determines the

greatness of ultimate *distinction.*

CHARLES KENDALL ADAMS

Excellence is not a skill.

It is an *attitude.*

RALPH MARSTON

Trust yourself.

Create the kind of self that

you will **be happy** to live with

all your life.

Make the most of yourself by

fanning the tiny, inner sparks

of **possibility** into flames

of **achievement.**

FOSTER C. MCCLELLAN

If you want to

succeed,

you should strike out

on ***new paths*** rather

than travel the worn paths

of accepted ***success.***

JOHN D. ROCKEFELLER

The person who

succeeds

is not the one who holds back,

fearing failure, nor the one

who never fails, but rather the one

who *moves on*

in spite of failure.

CHARLES R. SWINDOLL

Someone has well said,

"Success is a journey,

not a destination."

Happiness is to be found along the way,

not at the end of the road, for then

the journey is over and it is too late.

Today, this hour, this minute is *the day,*

the hour, the minute for each of us to sense

the fact that *life is good,* with all of its

trials and troubles, and perhaps more

interesting because of them.

ROBERT R. UPDEGRAFF

Twelve Priceless Qualities of Success

1. The *value* of time.

2. The *success* of perseverance.

3. The *pleasure* of working.

4. The *dignity* of simplicity.

5. The *worth* of character.

6. The *power* of kindness.

7. The *influence* of example.

8. The *obligation* of duty.

9. The *wisdom* of economy.

10. The *virtue* of patience.

11. The *improvement* of talent.

12. The *joy* of originating.

MARSHALL FIELD

Success

is not measured by what you

accomplish

but by the opposition

you have encountered,

and the *courage* with which

you have *maintained* the struggle

against overwhelming odds.

ORISON SWETT MARDEN

Be strong and do not give up,

for your work will be *rewarded.*

2 CHRONICLES 15:7

The **best advice** I can give to any young person upon **graduation from school** can be summed up in **exactly eight words,** and they are –

Be honest with yourself, and tell the truth.

JAMES A. FARLEY

Sound Advice for the Road Ahead

Make plans by seeking advice.

PROVERBS 20:18

Nothing in the world can take

the place of *persistence.*

Talent will not;

nothing is more common than

unsuccessful people with *talent.*

Genius will not;

unrewarded genius is almost a proverb.

Education will not;

the world is full of educated failures.

Keep believing,

keep trying.

Persistence and *determination*

alone are omnipotent!

CALVIN COOLIDGE

By *persistence*
the snail
reached the ark.

CHARLES H. SPURGEON

God gives every

bird a worm,

but He does not throw

it into the *nest.*

SWEDISH PROVERB

The great composer

does not set to work

because he is inspired,

but becomes inspired

because he is working.

Beethoven, Wagner, Bach, and Mozart

settled down day after day to the job in hand

with as much regularity as an accountant settles

down each day to his figures.

They didn't waste time

waiting for an inspiration.

ERNEST NEWMAN

Those who *build* the *future* are those who know that *greater things* are yet to come, and that they *themselves* will help bring them about. Their *minds* are illumined by the *blazing sun of hope.* They never stop to doubt. They haven't time.

MELVIN J. EVANS

Take a *lesson* from the mosquito:

he never waits for an *opening* –

he makes one.

Anonymous

Did you ever see an unhappy horse?

Did you ever see a *bird* that had the blues?

One reason why birds and horses

are not unhappy is because they

are not trying to *impress*

other birds and horses.

DALE CARNEGIE

" I will *give* you

what you *ask* for!

I will give you a

wise and

understanding heart."

1 KINGS 3:12 NLT

Teach us to

number our *days* aright,

that we may *gain*

a heart of *wisdom* .

PSALM 90:12

The *great thing* is to be found

at one's post as a *child of God,*

living each day as though it were our last,

but *planning* as though *our world*

might last a hundred years.

C. S. LEWIS

The future

lies before you

like a field of driven snow.

Be careful

how you tread it,

for every step will *show.*

ANONYMOUS

Celebrating You, Graduate!

*Oh, clap your hands,
all you peoples!
Shout to God with
the voice of triumph!*

PSALM 47:1 NKJV

You've paid your dues. Now go out there
and do something *remarkable!*

ANDREA GARNEY

Dear Graduate,

You have set a *high mark*

and achieved it.

Your reward is *expected and deserved.*

Even when you strained to *accomplish*

what was required you did not shrink back,

despising the *effort,*

but instead *pushed forward,*

pushed through.

In the years to come, you will look back

on this day with *sweet reflection,*

and a colorful *montage of memories*

touching the edges of *your mind.*

You step out now into the *future,*

better for having reached

this significant milestone.

I celebrate you!

My *favorite* memories of school are:

_____

_____

_____

_____

_____

_____

_____

_____

_____

_____

_____

The *most important lessons*
learned during my years of study are:

_____

_____

_____

_____

_____

_____

_____

_____

_____

_____

_____

I will *never forget* these wonderful friends:

_____

_____

_____

_____

_____

_____

_____

_____

_____

_____

_____